Treading the Ebony Path

Treading the

Ebony Path

Ideology and Violence
in Contemporary
Afro-Colombian Prose Fiction

Marvin A. Lewis

University of Missouri Press
Columbia, 1987

Copyright © 1987 by
The Curators of the University of Missouri
University of Missouri Press, Columbia, Missouri 65211
Printed and bound in the United States of America
All rights reserved

Library of Congress Cataloging-in-Publication Data
Lewis, Marvin A.

   Treading the ebony path.

   Bibliography: p.
   Includes index.
   1. Colombian fiction—20th century—History and criticism. 2. Colombian fiction—Black authors—History and criticism. 3. Alienation (Social psychology) in literature. 4. Violence in literature.
I. Title.
PQ8172.L49   1987   863   86-30901
ISBN 0-8262-0638-7 (alk. paper)

∞™ This paper meets the minimum requirements of
the American National Standard for Permanence of Paper
for Printed Library Materials, Z39.48, 1984.

For Judy, Monica, and Kevin—Latin lovers

Acknowledgments

Thanks to the Research Board of the University of Illinois for providing me with travel and research assistance and to the Research Council of the University of Missouri for typing support. Thanks to Rita Scott and Mrs. Addie Williams in Urbana for manuscript preparation and editorial assistance and to Donna Perry in Columbia for typing.

All translations from Spanish into English are my own.

M.A.L.
Columbia, Mo.
June 1, 1987

Contents

Acknowledgments, vii

1. Introduction, 1

2. Colombian Hunger:
   Arnoldo Palacios, 15

3. The Literary Synthesizer:
   Carlos Arturo Truque, 38

4. The Poet as Novelist:
   Jorge Artel and Juan Zapata Olivella, 63

5. From Oppression to Liberation:
   Manuel Zapata Olivella, 85

6. Conclusion, 120

Notes, 124

Bibliography, 131

Index, 139

1. Introduction

Between 1947 and 1983, five Colombian writers of African descent—Arnoldo Palacios, the late Carlos Arturo Truque, Jorge Artel, Juan Zapata Olivella, and his brother Manuel Zapata Olivella—published three volumes of short stories and eleven novels, in addition to dramas, essays, and poetry. Although their works are of high literary quality, and although all five have been mentioned in articles, portions of dissertations, and several book chapters, no one has examined the development of Afro-Colombian prose fiction as it is reflected in the works of all these authors.

This study situates these writers within the social, historical, and literary traditions of their country while, at the same time, scrutinizing their unique contributions as Afro-Colombian writers. My purpose is not to deny their Colombian ancestry or their cultural nationalism, but rather to place positive emphasis on the influence of their African heritage on their literary strategies. In most cases this latter aspect has been overlooked, partly because these writers do not write exclusively about the black experience in Colombia.

Following this Introduction, Chapter 2, "Colombian Hunger: Arnoldo Palacios," analyzes two novels, *Las estrellas son negras* (*The Stars Are Black*, 1949) and *La selva y la lluvia* (*The Jungle and the Rain*, 1958). Chapter 3, "The Literary Synthesizer: Carlos Arturo Truque," is devoted to two volumes of short stories, *Granizada y otros cuentos* (*Hailstorm and Other Stories*, 1953) and *El día que terminó el verano* (*The Day Summer Ended*, 1973). Chapter 4, "The Poet as Novelist: Jorge Artel and Juan Zapata Olivella," examines novels by two writers who earned their reputations as poets: *No es la muerte, es el morir . . .* (*It's Not Death, It's Dying*, 1979) by Artel, and *Historia de un joven negro* (*The Story of a Black Youth*, 1983) and *Pisando el camino de ébano* (*Treading the Ebony Path*, 1984) by Juan Zapata Olivella. Chapter 5, "From Oppression to Liberation: Manuel Zapata Olivella," evaluates six novels by one of Colombia's leading writers: *Tierra mojada* (*The Drenched Earth*,

1947), *La calle 10* (*10th Street*, 1960), *Chambacú Corral de negros* (*Chambacú, a Black Ghetto*, 1963), *Detrás del rostro* (*Behind the Mask*, 1963), *En Chimá nace un santo* (*In Chimá a Saint Is Born*, 1964), and *Changó, el gran putas* (*Changó, the Great SOB*, 1983). In my Conclusion I evaluate the importance of these writers within the Colombian narrative tradition as they relate to the concepts of ideology and violence.

The word *Afro-Colombian* is used in this study to suggest that these writers recognize the importance of their ethnic backgrounds in the development of their literary creations and in the manner in which they relate to Colombian society. They are faced with the task of writing both as Colombians and as blacks. This creates a unique problem of duality of perspective since they cannot separate the situation of poor blacks from that of the majority of destitute Colombians. Therefore, the issue in the literature becomes one of balancing class/caste against ethnicity, with the realization by the authors that, for Afro-Colombians, the class problem is compounded by one of color. The question then arises as to what extent the African background serves either to exacerbate or to alleviate social pressures.

In an informative article, Edward Kamau Brathwaite defines four types of written African literatures in the Caribbean: (1) rhetorical; (2) of African survival; (3) of African expression; and (4) of reconnection in ascending order of authenticity.[1] These categories vary from the rhetorical use of Africa "as a mask, a sign, or *nomen*" to the attempt by writers "to bridge the cultural gap with the spiritual earth mother" through literary expression, which is the intent of the literature of reconnection.

I assume that this conceptualization by Brathwaite is applicable to literature written by blacks throughout the Americas. For instance, these categories can be related to the African presence in the literature of contemporary Colombian writers of African descent, especially Jorge Artel and Manuel Zapata Olivella. The best example of literature of reconnection in the Americas is *Changó, the Great SOB* (1983) by Manuel Zapata Olivella, which interprets in epic fashion the black experience from the capture of prisoners in Africa to the death of Malcolm X in the United States.

Due to their separation by time and distance from their

African past, however, one cannot realistically expect Afro-Hispanic writers to constantly maintain a commitment to that past, to constantly search for positive values in an ethnic identity at the expense of national concerns. Richard Jackson has suggested a more feasible way for the black writer to address his literary craft to the plight of blacks and of the masses in Latin America. Jackson's thesis is that some of the most "authentic" Latin American literature is being produced by writers of African descent who are representative of the process of miscegenation in their countries and who are able to capture the human experiences of the majority from an insider's perspective rather than from the distant posture assumed by *criollo* writers of the elite class. Jackson maintains:

> In the first place, there is a corpus of literature by "realistically committed" black authors in Latin America, and since this is black literature written "from within" it is more authentic than the literary expression of concerned white humanists who, however sincere and humanistic in their advocacy, are still on the outside looking in. In fact, inauthenticity has been one of the major clichés critics have levelled against the social protest literature of the "old masters" who wrote about other people's lived experiences. Such accusations of inauthenticity can hardly be levelled at the black literature of Candelario Obeso, Nicolás Guillén, and Juan Pablo Sojo, for example, whose expressions of literary Americanism grow out of their own lived experiences. It has been said that the sense of honest identification Blacks bring to black writing is a necessary prerequisite for any truly authentic expression of the African heritage. And when that heritage is understood in its New World context, it becomes clear why black literature can best represent literary Americanism at its most genuine.[2]

The writers discussed in this study are exponents of literary Americanism who assess the plight of the majority of people in Colombia. The perspectives are those of Afro-Colombian authors who extend their craft to scrutinize the plight of the urban and rural dispossessed. The Zapata Olivellas, Truque, Artel, and Palacios do not limit themselves to the black experience; instead, they incorporate the *mestizo* population whose condition is similar to that of oppressed people throughout the Americas. This sense of "honest identification" allows them to interpret the Colombian milieu in a realistic fashion.

Out of necessity, Afro-Colombian literature espouses an ideology advocating a change in the existing social structures. This literary expression is a response to centuries of exploitation and domination in Colombia and the rest of Latin America. Jackson observes:

> The ultimate justification, however, for considering Afro-Latin American literature to be an alternative response to dependency in Latin America and an authentic model for literary Americanism is that this literature, written "from within," is literature that focuses, in part, on *la especificidad latinoamericana*. And when that literature deals with the black experience and is produced by those whose problems are under focus rather than by outside—however well-meaning—observers, the literary expression becomes a genuine example of "authentic communication," unblocked by obstacles of race, class and foreign vision that prevent even the most respected authors from seeing and understanding the cultures of the exploited in Latin America.[3]

From Manuel Zapata Olivella's *The Drenched Earth* (1947) to his monumental *Changó, the Great SOB* (1983), Afro-Colombian prose fiction has been an attempt to interpret *la especificidad latinoamericana*. The authors discussed here succeed in developing a Latin American ethnopoetics by "seeing and understanding the cultures of the exploited in Latin America" and by transforming their visions into literary creations.

The themes of alienation and exile are important in this regard. The sense of social estrangement felt by the writers themselves is bound to affect their presentation of character and circumstance. They experience what Max Dorsinville terms "the exile of being black in the world" and "the exile of the artist."[4] Another aspect of this phenomenon is inner exile, which according to Paul Ilie is "a term best confined to the disaffected sectors within the landed population as they relate to the official culture."[5] The relationship between Afro-Colombian writers and the "official culture" is basically one of alienation, marginality, and estrangement.

These writers place the blame for their disaffection squarely on the ruling minority. They emphasize, therefore, many negative elements in Colombian society.

My critical approach to this material is eclectic, utilizing a combination of formalist, culturalist, and historical-dialectical criticism. Out of necessity, this method involves analyses of style, structure, theme, myth, archetype, and ideology. On a broader scale, I examine some of the relationships between literature and society in the intrinsic and extrinsic evaluations of these texts. From a black perspective, my principal objectives are (1) to define the Afro-Colombian dimension of Colombian prose fiction; (2) to examine the literary manifestations of key social concepts such as identity, cultural dualism, psychic liberation, and societal confrontation; and (3) to give positive value to Colombian literary *negritud* in a society that more often than not seeks to deny its importance. My main hypothesis is that there is a sense of thematic and structural continuity in the literary expressions of these Afro-Colombian writers who are separated in time and space. This will be demonstrated through comparative/contrastive analyses of the texts utilizing broad (cultural) and narrow (literary) views of intertextuality.

Indeed, intertextuality, ideological violence, and authenticity are concepts germane to the study of Afro-Colombian literature. Any evaluation of this nature should address the interrelatability of "texts," to assess the author's world view and arrive at an understanding of the uniqueness of the Afro-Colombian literary perspective.

First of all, my understanding of intertextuality is based on the clear definition offered by Jonathan Culler, who comments on the "double focus" of this concept:

On the one hand, it calls our attention to the importance of prior texts, insisting that the autonomy of texts is a misleading notion and that a work has the meaning it does only because certain things have previously been written. Yet in so far as it focuses on intelligibility, on meaning, "intertextuality" leads us to consider prior texts as contributions to a code which makes possible the various effects of signification. Intertextuality thus becomes less a name for a work's relation to particular prior texts than a designation of its participation in the discursive space of a culture. The study of intertextuality is thus not the investigation of sources and influences as traditionally conceived; it casts its net wider to include anonymous discursive practices, codes whose origins are lost, that make possible the signifying practices of later texts.[6]

Texts, in the intertextual notion, are not limited to printed books. In Afro-Colombian literature there are common experiential images, from slavery to the present, that link the cultural experiences of these writers. This is most apparent in poetry treating the African experience and in Manuel Zapata Olivella's novel assessing the dispersion of blacks throughout the Americas. This concept, however, exists at a more complex level. What this group of writers accomplishes is a surfacing of some of the Afro-Colombian cultural codes, usually related to struggle, whose origins have been lost over the centuries, thereby demonstrating a commonality of experience that defies time. Exactly how this body of work participates in the discursive space of Colombian culture is one of my concerns.

Most Afro-Colombian literature is "social" in nature due to the historical role of blacks in Colombia. The writers consistently adapt the perspective of the societal underdogs with the idea of using literature to articulate many intolerable situations. Economics and politics are at the thematic core of the works discussed in this study, necessitating an examination of ideology in order to view how the fictional world interprets the inner dynamics of the real model upon which it is constructed.

For my purposes, the best discussions of ideology are found in the works of Raymond Williams and Terry Eagleton. Therefore, I will be using a combination of the ideas of these two critics in interpreting the social dimension of the texts. Eagleton claims: "Ideology is not in the first place a set of doctrines; it signifies the way men live out their roles in class-society, the values, ideas and images which tie them to their social functions and so prevent them from a true knowledge of society as a whole."[7] Raymond Williams points out that ideology "did not originate in Marxism" and distinguishes "three common versions of the concept":

Introduction

 (i) a system of beliefs characteristic of a particular class or group;
 (ii) a system of illusory beliefs—false ideas or false consciousness—which can be contrasted with true or scientific knowledge;
 (iii) the general process of the production of meanings and ideas.[8]

Eagleton and Williams offer similar definitions of ideology as it relates to power, domination, and class structure. Elsewhere Williams elaborates further on category (i) by stating that the world view expressed by a class or group "will include formal and conscious beliefs but also less conscious, less formulated attitudes, habits and feelings, or even unconscious assumptions, bearings and commitments."[9]

In addition, Catherine Belsey has set forth an excellent and useful discussion of the connection between literature and ideology. In her treatment of "The Subject in Ideology," a discussion of the different points of view advanced by Roland Barthes, Jacques Lacan, and Louis Althusser, Belsey comments:

The argument is not only that literature represents the myths and imaginary versions of real social relationships which constitute ideology, but also that classic realist fiction, the dominant literary form of the nineteenth century and arguably of the twentieth, "interpellates" the reader, addresses itself to him or to her directly, offering the reader as the position from which the text is most "obviously" intelligible, the position of the *subject in (and of) ideology*.[10]

Later in the discussion, Belsey adds: "Ideology suppresses the role of language in the construction of the subject. As a result, people 'recognize' (misrecognize) themselves in the ways in which ideology 'interpellates' them, or in other words, addresses them as subjects, calls them by their names and in turn 'recognizes' their autonomy."[11] The writers under discussion here are neorealists who succeed in "interpellating" the reader as subject. Ideologically, the reader reconstructs a fictional autonomous world representing the myths and imaginary versions of real social relationships inherent in Colombian society.

As manifested in their prose fiction, the ideological postures of the Afro-Colombian writers vary from overt calls for the implementation of Socialism in the works of Jorge Artel, Arnoldo Palacios, and Manuel Zapata Olivella to a subtle questioning of the values, ideas, and images that tie the privileged in Colombia to their social functions. These questions are thoroughly examined in the works of Carlos Arturo Truque and Juan Zapata Olivella, although their message is not as strident as that of their counterparts.

In discussing contemporary Colombian prose fiction, it is imperative to consider the question of violence. As a theme, violence permeates this literature and manifests itself in two ways. The first is reflected in the interpretations by Palacios, Artel, and Manuel Zapata Olivella of the historical assassination of the liberal leader Jorge Eliecer Gaitán on 9 April 1948, supposedly by conservative forces. This incident spawned not only unmitigated violence but also a body of literature offering multiple interpretations of the event.[12] The second involves the daily violence associated with human passions and the fight for survival as they are portrayed in the works of all these Afro-Colombian writers. This combination of historical and interhistorical destruction is one of the most pessimistic aspects of the literature.

My discussion of literary violence is based on the concepts advanced by Ariel Dorfman in his classic study on imagination and violence in America. "America is fruit of a prolonged violence, of a continuous pillage, of civil and fratricidal war in all of her geography," maintains Dorfman.[13] He outlines four basic categories of violence: vertical and social; horizontal and individual; nonspatial and interior; and narrative. The first two manifestations are most applicable to the works of the writers under consideration in this study.

1. LA VIOLENCIA VERTICAL Y SOCIAL
Los personajes, al darse cuenta de que son víctimas, se rebelan contra la sociedad que ha creado su situación, usando la violencia como una forma de liberación colectiva. Para construir se necesita

primero destruir, para la paz se hace la guerra, a la explotación directa se responde con la violencia directa. El hombre siente que, al hacerse histórica, su violencia cobra sentido; por ser vertical, dirigida contra los de arriba, como respuesta a la opresión, se piensa que se podrá controlar este tipo de agresividad. Pero es inevitable que estos héroes sean, finalmente, asesinados. Sus esfuerzos aislados son generalmente el producto de actos inconscientes más que el resultado de una postura organizada y racional. Una revolución no crece como las plantas, aunque la experiencia de lucha también ha demostrado que muchas veces la organización política frena el desarrollo de esa violencia.

2. LA VIOLENCIA HORIZONTAL E INDIVIDUAL
Estos personajes agreden a otro ser humano, a veces un amigo, o un miembro de su propia familia, otras veces a cualquiera que se le cruce por el camino: su violencia no tiene, para ellos, un claro sentido social, aunque la sociedad enajenante vibra como trasfondo invisible de todos sus actos aparentemente gratuitos y triviales. En la accidentalidad de su transcurrir, la evidencia es lo único necesario. Los llamamos horizontal porque luchan entre sí seres que ocupan un mismo nivel existencial de desamparo y de alienación: máquinas golpeadoras desatándose en contra de hermanos que son tratados como enemigos.[14]

1. VERTICAL AND SOCIAL VIOLENCE
The characters, upon realizing that they are victims, rebel against the society which has created their situation, using violence as a form of collective liberation. In order to build it is necessary first to destroy, for peace one makes war, to direct exploitation one responds with direct violence. Man feels that, upon becoming historical, his violence achieves meaning; by being vertically directed against those above, as an answer to oppression, he thinks that he will be able to control this type of aggressiveness. But it is inevitable that those heroes are, finally, assassinated. Their isolated efforts are generally the product of unconscious acts more than the result of an organized and rational posture. A revolution does not grow like plants, although the experience of struggle has demonstrated that many times political organization slows the development of that violence.

2. HORIZONTAL AND INDIVIDUAL VIOLENCE
These characters assault another human being, at times a friend, or a member of their own family, other times whoever crosses their

path: their violence does not have, for them, a clear social meaning, although alienating society vibrates as an invisible background to all their apparently gratuitous and trivial acts. In the accidentality of their happening, evidence is the only thing necessary. We call this horizontal because human beings fight among themselves, those who occupy the same existential level of helplessness and alienation: striking machines unraveling against brothers who are treated as enemies.

Vertical and horizontal violence are integral components of the world views projected by all these writers. As will be revealed in the analysis of works, these writers portray a constant struggle against oppressive social constraints and against neighbors. They also portray internal psychological battles and incorporate innovative narrative techniques into the fiction. Therefore, but to a lesser degree, nonspatial and narrative violence are also in evidence in the prose, although not at the same intensity.

In delineating the aforementioned categories of violence, Dorfman does not mention the novels of Arnoldo Palacios or Manuel Zapata Olivella as being exemplary of the destructive tendencies in Spanish-American literature. Instead, Gabriel García Márquez, the Colombian, and other Boom writers receive the brunt of his critical attention. As I will demonstrate, in both the rural and the urban contexts, Afro-Colombian writers are not only very effective in treating the theme of violence and its literary ramifications but also highly critical of the impact of violence on society.[15]

"La Violencia," which began in 1948 with the assassination of Gaitán, is a unifying structural concept in the works of these writers. As I have already noted, this episode of Colombian history is a recurring experiential image in the novels of Arnoldo Palacios, Jorge Artel, and Manuel Zapata Olivella. In addition, vertical/social violence is a major concern in *The Jungle and the Rain*, *10th Street*, and *It's Not Death, It's Dying*, while the horizontal variety plays havoc in *Hailstorm and Other Stories*, *The Day Summer Ended*, and *Behind The Mask*. Therefore, by discussing these two basic concepts, ideology and violence, it is possible to see what black writers contribute from both ethnic and national perspectives.

Afro-Colombian literature is an emerging area of scholarly investigation in the United States. To their credit, two major critics of Spanish-American literature, John Brushwood in *The Spanish American Novel: A Twentieth Century Survey* (1975) and Kessel Schwartz in *A New History of Spanish American Fiction* (1977), devote several pages to Afro-Colombian writers. Other standard studies of Spanish-American prose fiction, such as Gordon Brotherston's *The Emergence of the Latin American Novel* (1977) and Donald Shaw's *Nueva narrativa hispanoamericana* (1981), do not mention this important group of writers. On the other hand, Richard Jackson in his illuminating critical evaluations of Afro-Hispanic literature, *The Black Image in Latin American Literature* (1976) and *Black Writers in Latin America* (1979), provides an excellent introduction to some of the novels of Palacios and Manuel Zapata Olivella.

To date, no attempt has been made to discuss Afro-Colombian literature as a separate entity in the development of the national tradition. There have been, however, several serious efforts to include some of the Afro-Colombian fiction writers in discussions of the evolution of mainstream literature. These include doctoral dissertations by Barry Amis (1970) and Carl Pedersen (1971).[16] Amis focuses on *The Stars Are Black* as a naturalist work and treats *Chambacú, a Black Ghetto* as social protest literature. His objective is to "examine the theme of the Negro in the prose fiction of Colombia" from *Manuela* (1866) by Eugenio Díaz to *Chambacú, a Black Ghetto* (1963) by Manuel Zapata Olivella. Pedersen undertakes a more comprehensive survey, attempting "to fill the void left in the history of the Colombian novel since 1953." He treats dozens of novels published between 1954 and 1970 under the chapter headings "Rural," "Tropical," "Historical," "Urban," "Philosophical," "Psychological," "Cosmopolitan," and "Avant Garde." He discusses briefly *The Drenched Earth* and *In Chimá a Saint Is Born* as representative of novels of the "Ciclo Tropical." He analyzes *10th Street*, *Behind the Mask*, and *Chambacú, a Black Ghetto* in the chapter devoted to the "Historical Novel," recognizing that Manuel Zapata Olivella is an exponent of *literatura comprometida*. For Pedersen, the novels of

Zapata Olivella are representative of general tendencies in Colombian letters. He does not mention the works of Arnoldo Palacios.

The studies of both Amis and Pedersen build on earlier literary evaluations of the 1950s and 1960s such as Antonio Curcio Altamar's *Evolución de la novela colombiana* (*The Evolution of the Colombian Novel*, 1957), Humberto Bronx's *20 años de novela colombiana* (*20 Years of the Colombian Novel*, 1966), Gerardo Suárez Rondón's *La novela sobre la violencia en Colombia* (*The Novel of Violence in Colombia*, 1966), and Nestor Madrid-Malo's "Estado actual de la novela en Colombia" ("The Present State of the Novel in Colombia," 1967). The latter critic traces the development of the novel from *María* (1867) by Jorge Isaacs to *El hostigante verano de los dioses* (*The Haunting Summer of the Gods*, 1963) by Fanny Buitrago, with an adulatory evaluation of this genre's status during the decade of the 1960s:

> Tras haber visto así el panorama novelístico de Colombia en los últimos veinticinco años, con las necesarias referencias a los inmediatos y remotos antecedentes, ¿qué conclusiones pueden sacarse sobre la hora actual de nuestra novela y sobre las orientaciones que en ella predominan? Ante todo, es evidente que el nucleo más descollante—el constituido por los novelistas de primera línea; Mejía Vallejo, Zapata Olivella, García Márquez, Santa, Ponce de León, Soto Aparicio, Cepeda Samudio, Rojas Herazo, Fanny Buitrago—tanto por la calidad de la obra ya realizada como por las especiales dotes que para el cultivo de ese género han demostrado poseer todos ellos, asegura la plena y eficaz presencia de Colombia en el conjunto de la novela latinoamericana de hoy.[17]

After having viewed in this way the novelistic panorama of Colombia in the last twenty-five years, with the immediate and remote antecedents, what conclusions can be drawn about the present status of our novel and about the orientations that predominate in the genre? Above all, it is evident that the most outstanding nucleus— that constituted by the front-line novelists; Mejía Vallejo, Zapata Olivella, García Márquez, Santa, Ponce de León, Soto Aparicio, Cepeda Samudio, Rojas Herazo, Fanny Buitrago—as much for the quality of work already done as for the special talents for the cultivation of that genre all of them have been demonstrated to possess, assures the full and efficient presence of Colombia in the entirety of the Latin American novel today.

Manuel Zapata Olivella is included with the best contemporary Colombian novelists due to the excellent caliber of his work.

The point to be made here is that none of the studies mentioned seeks to define or discuss the commonality of prose fiction written by Afro-Colombian writers. On the other hand, I intend to demonstrate that the many thematic and conceptual similarities prevalent in these black writers affirm their ethnicity without negating their Colombian heritage. At the same time, although Palacios, Truque, Artel, and the Zapata Olivellas maintain an Afro-Colombian identity, they represent the majority point of view in their interpretations of Colombian reality. Psychological penetration and the ability to understand the different strata of Colombian society are the strong points of these writers. To a man, they concentrate on *la especificidad latinoamericana/colombiana*.

One of the major assumptions of this study is that, although these writers are of different generations and from different sections of their country, they are linked through the cultural experience of being black in a society that does not place much emphasis on the value of their racial heritage. What one perceives from reading this collection of prose fiction are human situations in which protagonists confront, in Eagleton's words, "the values, ideas and images which tie them to their social functions and so prevent them from a true knowledge of society as a whole." This search for truth and justice is continuous, but, in most works by Afro-Colombian writers, the dominant societal values prevail.

Violence is presented as an alternative by each of these writers. While there is implied criticism of in-group individual violence, well-directed vertical violence is presented as at least getting the attention of the oppressors. Dorfman's assertion that "America is the fruit of a prolonged violence, of a continuous pillage," is an attitude that is manifested by these authors and that serves as a structural link among their works.

The concept of cultural intertextuality is applicable to the degree that these writers present a black literary perspective based on experiences grounded in history and articulated in a manner that encompasses the majority of the poor in Colombia. These literary interpretations achieve meaning only when viewed in relation to the experiences of the have-nots or to other assessments of their existence.

Taken as a whole, these novels and short stories are representative both of general literary trends in Colombia and of the unique perspective presented by black writers. What is also consistent is the strong mode of social protest from 1947 to 1983. When the focus is on Afro-Colombians and the poor in general, neither the rural nor the urban environment offers solace for a population constantly under duress. There is unanimity by these authors in their call for revolution, a complete change in the existing social and economic orders. Realistically, this is not likely to occur. Violence and ideology, then, become the two rhetorical symbols that structure the literature of Afro-Colombian prose fiction writers of the second half of the twentieth century.

2. Colombian Hunger

Arnoldo Palacios

The Stars Are Black

In a recent international symposium devoted to the historical role of blacks in Colombia, a leading anthropologist stated:

A partir de 1950 el énfasis que he concedido a la antropología no significa de ninguna manera que la literatura de negros o sobre negros no siga siendo importante para los estudios sociales. Por el contrario, la creación literaria de escritores como Jorge Artel, Manuel Zapata Olivella, Marco Realpe Borja, Helcías Martán Góngora, Hugo Salazar Valdés, y otros poetas y novelistas de generaciones más recientes como Yvonne Truque enriquece la continuidad del proceso iniciado por Obeso hace cerca de cien años.[1]

After 1950 the emphasis that I have conceded to anthropology does not mean in any way that literature by blacks or about blacks does not continue being important for the social sciences. On the other hand, the literary creations of writers like Jorge Artel, Manuel Zapata Olivella, Marco Realpe Borja, Helcías Martán Góngora, Hugo Salazar Valdés, and other poets and novelists of more recent generations such as Yvonne Truque enrich the continuity of the process initiated by Obeso nearly one hundred years ago.

An important, neglected figure in this equation is Arnoldo Palacios, who offers one of the first profound contemporary interpretations of Afro-Colombians from a fictional perspective.

Arnoldo Palacios belongs to what John Brushwood calls the Generation of "24": those writers born between 1894 and 1924 whose period of predominance in literature fell during the years 1924–1954.[2] Palacios was born in Cértegui, in the Chocó region, on 20 January 1924, and his first major novel,

The Stars Are Black, was published in 1949. He is, therefore, of the same Spanish-American literary generation as Miguel Angel Asturias, Agustín Yáñez, Leopoldo Marechal, and Alejo Carpentier. However, Palacios's other important novel, *The Jungle and the Rain* (1958), places him within the pre-Boom period of 1956–1962.

Any attempt to come to grips with the literary world of Arnoldo Palacios has to take into account the ideological content of this writer's works, not just because of his political posture but also because of the Colombian forces that interact in the novels. In his works, Palacios strives to illustrate how the dominant ideology affects character relationships and individual perceptions in the fictional world. He is concerned both with how the "system of beliefs characteristic of a particular class or group" mitigates circumstances as well as with "the general process of the production of meanings and ideas."[3] Palacios narrates from the perspective of the downtrodden masses in an effort to demonstrate how social forces limit their ability to surmount such obstacles as color and class. There is a constant struggle on the part of blacks and the poor to overcome the historical biases and attitudes that are imposed by the ruling class in an effort to negate the self-worth and dignity of the less fortunate. Therefore, both vertical and horizontal violence are integral thematic elements in Palacios's works.

Arnoldo Palacios is well versed in literary theory and its application to fiction. His novels, therefore, can bear diverse critical readings from the perspectives of both technique and content. *The Stars Are Black* can be read as a "naturalist" work, while *The Jungle and the Rain* lends itself more to an ideological analysis. Together, these novels present an interpretation of a people and its culture from the point of view of an insider who bears witness to decades of toil and suffering.

Certainly, a great deal of Afro-Colombian literature is bound up with the historic patterns of economic and social oppression that blacks have undergone from slavery to the present. Both of Palacios's novels are attempts to interpret the particulars of this general experience. The ideological content of the novels is important also from the point of view of Palacios's personal life: he is a self-exiled writer now living in Europe whose second novel, *The Jungle and the Rain*, was first published in the Soviet Union. In his works Palacios interprets, rather than merely reflects, the experiences of impoverished blacks of the Chocó, and he does so with a degree of literary commitment that is bound to sway the reader. Therefore, in any interpretation of the novels of Arnoldo Palacios the concepts of ideology and political commitment and their relationship to world view are essential considerations.

Both of Palacios's novels treat the context of the Chocó from the perspective of the underdog, primarily the black Chocoan population and its struggle for survival against insurmountable natural and human obstacles. Poverty, misery, injustice, and the unending human struggle for change are at the thematic core of Palacios's works. When *The Stars Are Black* was first published, it received an enthusiastic review from Alvaro Monroy. With a great deal of compassion, he wrote:

Palacios no podía traicionarse ni traicionar a sus hermanos de raza, a los mismos con quienes compartió la niñez y la adolescencia; aquellos que no tienen otra esperanza de redención que la de su Dios, y viven, crecen y mueren en su mundo circundado de miseria, de hambre, de desprecio y de prejuicios raciales.[4]

Palacios could not betray himself nor betray his racial brothers, the same ones with whom he shared childhood and adolescence; those who do not have another hope of redemption other than that of their God, and they live, grow up, and die in their world surrounded by misery, hunger, scorn, and racial prejudices.

Through his perceptive comments in this review, it is evident that Monroy is familiar with Palacios and his literary origins. In addition, he is sensitive to the interpretation of reality presented by the author.

Vicente Pérez Silva refers to this novel as "one of the most representative novels of Colombian literature."[5] On the other hand, Humberto Bronx states: "Arnoldo Palacios, in *The Stars Are Black* (1949), gave indications of a sordid and vile naturalism, uncommon and almost unique in Colombian literature."[6] This novel has been labeled a "naturalist" work by others as well, but none perceived it in as negative a light as did Bronx.

The critical assumption of this study is that *The Stars Are Black* contains some naturalist elements but resists such a strict classification because of its world view and narrative perspective. The understanding of the naturalist novel expounded here is based on the cogent explication of naturalist theory outlined by Lillian Furst and Peter Skrine, who comment:

> The Naturalist novel is one in which an attempt is made to present with the maximum objectivity of the scientist the new view of man as a creature determined by heredity, milieu and the pressures of the moment. . . . It is vital to realize that true literary Naturalism is at least as much a question of method as of subject; only when the writer treats his subject with the objectivity of the analytical scientist, can we speak of Naturalism.[7]

Palacios does not reach the degree of objectivity outlined by Furst and Skrine due to his closeness to the situation he is interpreting. His feelings for the Chocó and the region's people do not allow him to transcend his subjectivity to engage in scientific analysis. On the other hand, it is clear that "heredity, milieu, and the pressures of the moment" are the most important factors in the final destinies of Palacios's protagonist. These notions will form an important part of this discussion.

The Stars Are Black examines the impact of poverty on a family of five children, headed by a female, in one of Colombia's most remote and neglected regions. The children are two boys, Israel, the main protagonist, and his brother, Jesús, and three girls, Elena, Clara, and Aurora. They are faced with a tremendous battle for survival, through a hand-to-mouth existence, in a social environment where being black is not an asset. This novel is divided into four books: "Hambre," "Ira," "Nive," and "Luz Interior." The physical location is Quibdó, capital of the Chocó region, and its environs along the Atrato River. Irra, the novel's focal point, is consumed by two forces, hunger and rage—hunger to satisfy the physical necessity of nutrition, and rage at the conditions to which he and his people are subjected. *The Stars Are Black* presents Israel's thoughts and actions for a day, covering in its different sections the different moods that he experiences and his psychological and physical presence.

"Hambre" (Hunger), the first section of *The Stars Are Black*, reflects an agonizing attempt by Israel to bring order to his chaotic world, which is populated by disjointed images of suffering. Israel exists in a totally negative physical environment. There is not a positive word or description uttered in reference to people or physical reality. There is, however, concern with degradation and bodily functions.

Israel begins the first part of his literary day with an unsuccessful attempt to fish for food and ends it in a compromising and demeaning situation with homosexual overtones with don José, proprietor of a grocery store. The initial description of the old fisherman with whom Irra begins his day is not only one of abject poverty and misery; there is also the strong suggestion that life's chances have not been fair. The fisherman is described as having "cierto desprecio por lo pasajero y fútil, recia responsabilidad ante la vida larga que lo habia fustigado desde el momento en que le regalo el primer rayo de luz" (certain disdain for the ordinary and futile, strong responsibility before the long life that had rebuked him from the moment he had been given the first ray of light).[8] Consequently, his physical appearance reflects the amount of collective suffering with which the old-timer has been confronted. Irra, too, seems to be consumed by the feeling that somehow heredity is related to their current situation: "El había nacido para arrastrarse siempre como una tortuga . . . para arrastrarse y enredarse en su propia baba como las lombrices" (He was born to always drag himself along like a turtle . . . to crawl and entangle himself in his own slime like worms; p. 81).

By drawing these analogies with other forms of animal life, the narrator is able to establish a correlation between humans and nonhumans in the "naturalist's" definition of things. For instance, the emphasis on bodily functions, the individual personality at a biological level, is evident throughout *The Stars Are Black*. Snot, urine, and fecal matter play an important part in the relationship between humans and nature in this novel, certainly in developing a base presentation of human behavior.

For example, in his initial encounter with the oldster, Irra "se apretó el vientre y luchaba por vomitar. Hasta que fue saliendo una cosa verde, viscosa, que sabía amarga" (squeezed his stomach and fought to vomit. Until out flowed a green viscous substance that tasted bitter; p. 31). This expression of Israel's bodily "humor" would be applicable even within the classical mode. Later, Irra "se bajó los calzones y poniéndose en cuclillas . . . pujó. Algo se descargaba sobre la arena como blandojas pelotas de barro. Se asomó abajo y observó los puntales chorreadas de masa reseca, poblada de moscas" (dropped his pants and squatting . . . pushed. Something fell on the sand like small pellets of clay. He glanced below and observed the spurted dots of dried dough, covered with flies; p. 40). Still later, the focus on bodily functions is reflected by a shopkeeper who is blowing his nose: "hurgaba y hurgaba la nariz, y se entregaba a ello en cuerpo y alma, hasta el punto de que cerraba los ojos y abría la boca, por la cual fluía un hilo de baba. Al fin el hombre sacó el dedo de la nariz; adherido al dedo salió un moco duro, negruzo, que el tendero llevó a la boca casi inconscientemente" (He picked and picked his nose, and became involved in it body and soul, to the point that he closed his eyes and opened his mouth, from which a thread of spittle flowed. Finally the man pulled his finger from his nose; attached to his finger came a hard, black snot ball that the storekeeper put into his mouth almost unconsciously; p. 48). These vivid descriptions are clear indications of the naturalist tendencies of the novel.

Furst and Skrine have written in this regard:

In the development of Naturalism Darwin's theory is without doubt the most important single shaping factor. The Naturalist's view of man is directly dependent on the Darwinian picture of his descent from the lower animals. In contrast to the idealization of many by the Romantics, the Naturalists deliberately reduce him to animal level, stripping him of higher aspirations.[9]

Palacios's protagonists are far from being idealized. In fact, they are presented at the lowest moments of their existence. In both their conduct and their self-perceptions, Palacios's protagonists display naturalist tendencies in their everyday behavior and in their mimicry of other animals. This is evident in their never-ending quest to satisfy bodily functions and instinctual drives.

The hunger motif is developed to its fullest in the first section of *The Stars Are Black*. It is the physical sensation of not having enough to eat that drives Israel to the brink of criminal activity. "Hambre. Como era possible tanto tiempo sin comer?" (Hunger. How was it possible so much time without eating? p. 31) is the first reaction Irra has to his most vital preoccupation. Subsequently, analogies are drawn with a stray dog: "Perro flaco, hambriento. Perro desnutrido como la gente de allí, sin savia en el organismo, como savia no tenía las plantas durante el verano. Tampoco valía la vida siendo perro o gato o gallina" (A skinny, hungry dog. A malnourished dog like the people from here, without sap in the organism, just as plants do not have sap during the summer. Neither did life have value being a dog or cat or chicken; p. 47). Interestingly enough, this nonhuman analogy is an advancement over those in which Irra views himself in slime as if he were a turtle or worm. His only alternative is to exact justice for himself since the All Powerful has abandoned the poor: "Hay que matar" (One must kill), he shouts (p. 59).

The theme of being forsaken by God is developed fully throughout this first book. "Tampoco Dios se acuerda de los pobres" (Nor does God remember the poor) is constantly in the mind of Irra. Only slowly do readers become aware that Irra has indeed tried to help himself and his family but that prejudice and racism have impeded his progress toward finding a job. "¿Qué habia hecho el para sufrir tanto?" (What had he done to suffer so much?) prefigures and sets the tone for most of the action in "Ira" (Anger), the second part of *The Stars Are Black*. This section is designed to demonstrate the profound rage felt by Israel vis-à-vis his situation of poverty. The humiliation he feels on being turned down for a job for no apparent reason, resulting in his inability to contribute anything to the family's material well-being, is of utmost importance. The in-group violence that accompanies this type of impotence manifests itself at the dinner table when Israel, out of frustration, throws his plate into Aurora's face.

The scene develops in the following manner:

—¡Qué no me vea así, Elena!—profirió Irra . . . ¡Si quiere mi comida, jártesela! . . .

Elena gruñó retorciéndose, y se escurrió temerosa, debajo de la mesa. Tenía el rasguño de cuando Irra la pateó, por la tarde. Ahora querría azotarla de nuevo.

—¿Pol qué soj así con tuj helmanita, hombre?—Murmuró la madre, angustiada.

—Es el Patas—asintió, chillona Aurora.

—¡Qué no me jodan más, carajo! . . . ¡Váyanse a la porra!—gritó Irra, descargando el plato sobre la frente de Aurora. Los vidrios se desperdiciaron, y llovió arroz en la cocina. Irra se levantó azotando el asiento contra la pared. El asiento maltrecho se desarmó. (p. 108)

"Don't look at me that way, Elena!" uttered Irra . . . "If you want my food, stuff yourself! . . . "

Elena grunted retreating, and slipped away fearful, beneath the table. She had the scratch from when Irra kicked her in the afternoon. Now he wanted to beat her again.

"Why are you like that with your little sister, man?" his mother muttered, distressed.

"He is the Devil" added Aurora screaming.

"Don't fuck with me anymore, dammit! Go to hell!" shouted Irra, throwing the dish in Aurora's face. The pieces of glass splattered and rained rice over the kitchen. Irra jumped up throwing his chair against the wall. The battered seat fell apart.

Ironically, Israel does not direct his violent acts toward those most responsible for the family's situation. He only dreams of confronting the government and those in power while actually brutalizing his own family. The violence here is both physical and verbal, aimed at terrorizing his own. In addition to beating his sister and destroying the little furniture they have, Israel uses language that is charged with destruction and rage. Not only does he disrespectfully demand his food but he also curses his family in language more fit for the male domain. This is precisely the type of horizontal violence in which family members are treated like the enemy that I outlined at the beginning of this study.

Also, we learn here that Israel is not totally lacking in ambition, since he does aspire to an education, and his family does hold him in high regard. After all, in spite of his violent behavior, Israel is the first-born son, who has the responsibility of providing for his family. The family, too, is engaged in the struggle for survival, with Jesús, the fourteen-year-old as an exemplary figure of the hard-working and ambitious son. Israel, it seems, is at the juncture of manhood and not sure in which direction to go. The suffering, misery, and poverty weigh so heavily on him because he knows that there is a better way.

"¡Nive!," the third book, named after a female character, is the least congruous of the four sections in many ways. Its emphasis is on passion and sexual urges, which once satisfied end in tragedy, since Nive "dies" after her sexual union with Israel. This episode is also treated within the larger context of *mestizaje*, or miscegenation. The common level of suffering experienced by the protagonists does not diminish the strong preoccupation with ethnicity in the society:

Nive era la naturaleza human salvaje, más la sangre exótica, civilizada y dinámica. "Yo el negro de aquí. Ella la mulata." La voz de la tierra le gritaba a Irra acerca del imperio de la fusión de las sangres. (p. 132)

Nive was human savage nature, and more exotic, civilized, and dynamic blood. "I the black man from here. She the mulatta." The voice of the earth shouted to Irra about the dominion of the fusion of bloods.

Pigmentocracy is definitely an issue in *The Stars Are Black*, just as it is in Colombian society. Israel is aware not only of the rift between blacks and whites but also of the lesser tension between *mulatos* and *negros*. This is very much on his mind when he intends to have sexual relations with Nive. She reminds him that her mother "ha dicho que para verme casada con un negro preferiría verme tendida en una mesa con cuatro velas encenidiadas" (has said that to see me married to a black man, she would prefer to see me stretched out on a table with four lighted candles; p. 139). Since it is desirous to marry one who has a lighter skin, marriage to Irra instead will assure Nive's position in the lower echelon of society. There is some doubt, however, cast upon the episode between Irra and Nive due to the fact that the reader is not sure whether she actually dies or if her death is merely a part of Israel's imagination.

In true Darwinist fashion, hunger, rage, and sex are three of the natural impulses that Israel is seeking to satisfy. In spite of his miserable physical condition, his sexual urge has not declined. He is constantly thinking of the prostitutes he has experienced and desiring to participate in such activities again. It is, however, in the encounter with Nive that these desires are best manifested:

Violento impulso sexual le erizó el cuerpo a Irra. (p. 127)

A violent sexual impulse bristled Irra's body.

Tal vez Nive estaba buena. Profunda sacudida sensual le alborotó el organismo. (p. 130)

Perhaps Nive was good. A profound sensual jolt aroused his member.

¿Por qué diablos temblaba? ¿Resultados de instintos sexuales? (p. 131)

Why in the world was he trembling? The results of sexual instincts?

After Israel has satiated his sexual appetite, Nive supposedly dies of a mysterious ailment that he interprets as divine punishment. Her mother is of the opinion that she dies as a result of hunger and an unidentified stomach ailment. This situation is compounded by the fact that the doctor, who is drunk and at a party, is unavailable. This entire incident appears to Israel while he is in a dreamlike state, parallel to the situation in which he imagines the death of a local official. The reader learns later that Israel is contemplating a future with Nive, and the entire episode remains unclear at the novel's end.

"Luz Interior" (Interior Light), the final section of *The Stars Are Black*, is the key segment in which Irra decides not to leave home but to stay and try to overcome the social circumstances. This is indeed an ironic twist since throughout the text his situation is presented as unbearable. The model for success has been there all along, but Israel has failed to recognize it until he experiences a final revelation in which the poor people seem to be in charge of their own destinies because they survive with what they have:

Los campesinos subían desde la orilla con huevos, racimos de plátanos, chontaduro, pescados, piñas. Cada cual hacía lo que podía. Irra también haría. (p. 178)

The country people climbed up from the shores with eggs, stalks of bananas, chontaduro, fish, pineapple. Each one did what he could. Irra would also do it.

Israel's discovery takes place, significantly, near water, which symbolizes the unconscious, purification, and redemption. Concretely, this image is a cleansing and liberating force for a troubled mind. It is doubtful, however, that Israel will accept the status quo, since he knows there is more to life than the daily humiliations he and the members of his family suffer.

For Israel and his people the color of the stars, signifying their perception of the universe, is likely to remain static. In *The Stars Are Black*, because Palacios identifies so closely with the people of his region, there is not a convincing mesh of the interpretation of heredity, milieu, and the pressures of the moment with the narrative objectivity of the analytical scientist. Instead, the reader receives a very emotional rendering of a set of social circumstances experienced by the majority of blacks in the Chocó, Colombia's forgotten region. Palacios's cry was, and still is, for change. While *The Stars Are Black*, his first novel, posits a set of disheartening circumstances, *The Jungle and the Rain* analyzes the possibility of a solution.

The Jungle and the Rain

The Jungle and the Rain did not receive any of the positive accolades extended to Palacios's first novel. The reviewer in *Cromos* concluded:

> Al cerrar el libro, preferimos pensar que, antes que una novela auténtica, lo que acabamos de leer no es sino una serie de notas, de cuadros, de esbozos, todo ello mero material en bruto para la ulterior estructuración de un bello y revelador libro que habría de llevar por título el mismo de este esquema: *La selva y la lluvia*.[10]

> Upon closing the book, we prefer to think that rather than an authentic novel what we have just finished reading is nothing more than a series of notes, of pictures, of sketches, all of it mere raw material for the later structuring of a beautiful and revealing book that would bear the same title as this outline: *The Jungle and the Rain*.

The reviewer does give Palacios credit, however, for writing a work whose purpose is to "to convey to uninformed readers a realistic image of the physical, moral, and intellectual misery of our people and, especially, the situation of the people of color who inhabit our Pacific Coast." *The Jungle and the Rain* is an extension of *The Stars Are Black* to the degree that it treats the same geographic area; however, it encompasses a broader segment of the population.

The Jungle and the Rain begins as a Bildungsroman of the selva, the Chocó region of Colombia, and ends as "public service" literature. This novel's early focus is on the family of Gaspar, a forty-year-old man who barely survives in the gold-mining industry of this locale. The family consists of his wife and his children, Pedro José, Rosalbina, Carlitos, and Toño. They are defined in relation to the extreme poverty of the Chocó, which reinforces misery, self-hate, hunger, and despair. Consequently, there is a lack of communication that results in a profound degree of solitude and estrangement in a natural context that is not respectful of human existence. The family is faced with the stress of economic survival in an unyielding physical environment.

The Jungle and the Rain focuses on the trajectories of several central characters, Pedro José, Baltasar alias "Caimacán," and Luis Aníbal, all black products of the Chocó. None is able to have an impact on the country's social structures and consequently to better his own lot. The novel is schematic in that it follows different characters, shifts points of view, and does not resolve all individual destinies. Pedro José becomes a frustrated schoolteacher, Luis Aníbal becomes an intellectual Marxist, and Caimacán resists the status quo to the point of taking up arms against the oppressors.

The action has two dramatically distinct poles: the rural Chocó and urban Bogotá. For impoverished blacks and the poor masses, neither locale holds the opportunity for their collective advancement. Poverty, hunger, misery, and injustice are the most prevalent motifs as the novel covers a time span of approximately twenty years from 1930 to 1950.

The Jungle and the Rain is divided into six chapters. The fifth segment, which is central to the novel's world view, transpires in Bogotá, while the rest of the action takes place in the Chocó region. The novel initially focusus on ten years in the life of Pedro José, from the time he leaves home in dishonor, after losing the family's grocery money in the river, to his triumphant return as a *maestro*. The conceptual basis of the novel involves an assessment of the poor and how they are inhibited by both political and economic forces that stifle their chances to become something other than underdogs.

In chapter 5, *The Jungle and the Rain* reaches its culmination as a work that incorporates liberal ideas in reaction to the conservativism that surrounded the violence of 1948. Bogotá, the capital, is the scene of unrest and bloodshed due to the clash between the two opposing factions. The common people are caught in the middle, and the enlightened ones, such as Luis Aníbal, are instruments of misdirected energy more than they are effective agents for social change. At this point in the novel, the primary focus is political rather than economic, but the two are inseparable.

Combined with the exploitative tendencies of Colombian social forces—the Church, the military, and the oligarchy— is the specter of United States domination of this region through the Chocó Pacific Mining Company. There are several images of *gringos* in the novel, but their impact is made known to Pedro José by a boatowner with whom Pedro hitches a ride:

El sabía muy bien que esas lanchas eran de los norteamericanos, dueños, además, de esas dragas enormes que sacan el oro y el platino. Todo mundo allí había llegado a odiar a esa gente perversa. Aquella frase mascullada, "malditos, gringos," revoloteaba en la mente, inexperta todavía, pero maliciosa, del joven fugitivo.[11]

He knew very well that those barges were those of the North Americans, owners, beside, of those enormous dredges that take out gold and platinum. Everybody there had begun to hate those perverse people. That muttered phrase "damn gringos" fluttered in the memory, yet inexperienced, but malicious, of the fleeing youngster.

Pedro's apprenticeship involves becoming aware of the relationships between the exploiters and the exploited, a realization that would not have been possible for him had he remained at home. Pedro learns his lessons of social dynamics well, but to no avail. In the final analysis, one individual, he discovers, can do little to change the social structure, since the plight of the Chocoans is exacerbated by outside economic influence, in this case a multinational corporation.

The Chocó Pacífico, an affiliate of the South American Gold Company (actually of the International Mining Company of New York), in 1916 consolidated efforts begun in 1890 to exploit the riches of the San Juan River and its environs, including the tributary Condoto River. The Chocó Pacífico was a multinational operation with a token home office in a Colombian city and its real headquarters in New York, where all corporate business was conducted. Exploitation took place in Colombia, while the profits flowed to the United States. The impact of the company on the local population was devastating.

In his study on Condoto and the Chocó Pacific, Aquiles Escalante quotes a newspaper report by Gabriel García Márquez, who maintains:

La Compañía anda por los ríos con sus gigantes dragas extrayendo el oro y el platino y esterilizando con el cascote las tierras de la ribera. Todo esto, sumado a la pobreza de la población que se siente dueña de sus metales, que sabe de memoria las leyes y las interpreta a su manera, mientras ve correr sus grandes ríos despojados, ha contribuido a crear en la zona minera del Chocó un ambiente de injusticia y amargura que pesa en el aire, que se puede tocar con las manos en Cascote, Condoto, en Novita y Tadó, a todo lo largo y lo ancho del dilatado y empobrecido reino del platino.[12]

The Company goes along the rivers with its gigantic dredges extracting gold and platinum and sterilizing with the residue the lands of the riverbank. All that, added to the poverty of the population that feels itself owner of its metals while it sees its great rivers plundered, has contributed to create in the mining zone of the Chocó an environment of injustice and bitterness which weighs in the air, which one can touch with the hands in Cascote, Condoto, in Novita and Tadó, far and wide in the expanded and impoverished platinum kingdom.

In *The Jungle and the Rain*, although Gaspar's family does not know the direct source of its misery, it is apparent that the ability of family members to eke out a living is impaired by the presence of the mining company. Granted, a small number of jobs is provided, but this does not compensate for the people who are uprooted and unable to earn a traditional living in farming and mining. The ecological devastation of this region by the mining company compounds the human poverty and suffering experienced by its residents. Neither agriculture nor livestock raising is feasible due to the destruction of arable soil. The entire economic base of the San Juan River has been undermined by a force that, as a source of survival for the few, causes dependency on its very existence.

Pedro José migrates from Istmina to Quibdó early in the novel and realizes before long that the political circumstances that are tearing the country apart are incomprehensible for someone such as himself who is so far away, even though he is affected so profoundly by the government. Pedro José experiences a degree of rage, but he does not know toward whom to direct his fury. He surmises:

Había vivido en la selva casi al par que las bestias. Evocar ese pasado amargo, trágico, lo inundaba de odio hacia algo, hacia alguien que sin embargo no localizaba con precisión. Tal vez el 'Gobierno' precisamente . . . No comprendía bien: existían aquí dos bandos de liberales y el partido conservador. Los godos querían tomarse el poder: los liberales mandaban . . . 'empero, nosotros, pase lo que pasare, somos los perseguidos, vegetamos en la miseria, aun siendo liberales.' (pp. 64–65)

He had lived in the jungle almost on the level of the beasts. To evoke that bitter, tragic past filled him with hate toward something, toward someone who nevertheless he could not pinpoint with precision. Perhaps the "Government" precisely . . . He did not understand well: here there existed two bands of liberals and the conservative party. The conservatives wanted to take power for themselves: the liberals were ruling . . . "nevertheless, we, be that as it may, we are the persecuted, we wallow in misery, even being liberals."

This passage is the key to the novel's thematic and ideological thrust. Pedro José is now a literate black who tries to reflect on existential questions such as meaning and destiny. His confusion resides in the fact that when one has been kept at the level of starvation for most of one's life, official structures mean absolutely nothing. Liberal and conservative are merely two abstract notions that have not improved the situation for members of his family, who still live as beasts in the jungle, persecuted, in misery with a vague notion of being "liberals." In this case an anonymous officialdom exercises control over Pedro José and those of similar circumstances without regard for individuals. This political contradiction underscores the confusion experienced by the masses.

The fact that Pedro José has accomplished as much as he has is correctly interpreted by him as a personal triumph of monumental proportions: "se convenció de que al fin y al cabo su entrada al colegio había sido un triunfo más sobre esa vida y ese universo, empecinados en serle siempre hostiles" (he convinced himself that in the end his entrance to the school had been one more triumph over that life and that universe, stubborn in being always hostile to him; p. 65). Whether there is a cosmic conspiracy or whether the problem resides in Bogotá is beyond the comprehension of Pedro

José. He will suffer because he is poor, black, and unable to control his own destiny.

The lack of clarification concerning the differences between liberals and conservatives and the tensions within each group culminates in the modern epoch of "La Violencia," which erupts in April 1948 with the assassination of Gaitán. In *The Jungle and the Rain* this epoch is immediately preceded by strikes, social dissidence, and mass migration to the capital due to the economic situation. Much of the spontaneous involvement in the violence is told from the perspectives of Aminta (who has migrated from the *llano* for economic reasons), Luis Aníbal, and Julio Matiz. Aminta dies in the fighting; although she is involved early in anti-government propaganda, at the decisive moment "Amita no podía comprender cómo en un momento hubiese ya tanto muerto en la calle" (Amita could not understand how in an instant there had already been so much death in the street; p. 139). For his part, "Luis Aníbal ya no pensaba sino en accionar su fusil" (Luis Aníbal now thought of nothing except firing; p. 139). Matiz also suffers a rude awakening that is divorced from romantic aspects of the battle: "La vista de un almacén saqueado a cuya puerta un hombre muerto a cuchilladas, le produjo una tristeza amarga. Empero, él debía entender que el pueblo lo hizo por hambre también" (The sight of a looted store, with a squatting dead man in the door, produced a sad bitterness in him. Nevertheless, he had to learn that the people also did it for hunger; pp. 141-42). Although the young people who consider themselves revolutionaries have their political motives, from a practical standpoint economics is what determines the activities of most of the destitute masses involved. Luis Aníbal finally raises some pertinent, though rhetorical, questions:

¿Cuándo estallará la revolución para fundar aquí el socialismo? Eso no lo sabemos. ¿Luchar, repartir una docena de periódicos a mimeógrafo, pegar un cartel que la policía arrancaba immediatamente? ¿ . . . Dedicarle su vida entera a eso, sin saber exactamente cuándo se realizaría la revolución? (pp. 147-48)

When will the revolution to found socialism explode here? That we do not know. To fight, pass out a dozen mimeographed newspapers, put up a poster that the police immediately tore up? . . . Dedicate your entire life to that, without knowing exactly when the revolution would come about?

What Luis Aníbal, Aminta, and Matiz had hoped for disintegrates into random violence whose impact is felt throughout the country. Here, acts of disobedience are viewed as meaningless. Socialism is not an alternative, at least not from the perspective of Leonor Soto and her family, who view the masses as despicable and incapable of sharing in the wealth of Colombia. A complete change in the social and economic structure, a revolution, will not transpire as long as there is such a cultural and ideological breach among the social classes.

What was intended to be vertical violence against the ruling oppressors results in random killing in which the unorganized poor massacre themselves, not for social change, but for food. The wealthy are far removed from the fury of this insurrection. This is the central irony of *The Jungle and the Rain*.

The Jungle and the Rain is imbued with a great deal of revolutionary rhetoric. This is due both to the characters' perceptions of social injustices and to the world view of the novel. "Además ahí tienes a los gringos como una sanguijuela en nuestro pellejo . . . Aquí se necesita una revolución" (Besides here we have the gringos like a leech in our hide . . . Here we need a revolution; p. 83) is the assertion of Matiz, whose obsession is to organize a union at the Chocó Pacific Company. He exclaims:

—El aspecto de la empresa minera norteamericana Chocó-Pacífico, ahí me tiene un problema del cual nosotros nos hemos ocupado muy poco, casi nada—dijo Matiz, como haciéndose un reproche personal. —¡Como es posible que no exista allá un sindicato! (pp. 127-28)

"The aspect of the North American mining enterprise, Chocó Pacific, creates a problem for me here which we have paid little attention to, almost nothing," said Matiz, as if affronting himself personally. "How is it possible that a union does not exist over there!"

All attempts to organize the proletariat are thwarted by the political forces in power. Violence, the last alternative for change, is not the answer either. This is made clear in the novel as Caimacán, one of the exponents of violence, is being pursued by the forces of law and order at the end of *The Jungle and the Rain*. His revolutionary compatriots have been decimated. Recognizing his serious miscalculation, Caimacán questions,

¿y quién sabe cuánta más gente habrá caído, estará cayendo, estará siendo detenida para pudrirse en la cárcel por mi culpa . . . Ser revolucionario no es apenas ser un hombre de cojones . . . Hay que poseer una cabeza que sepa por donde va el agua al molino . . . El que ignorante peca, ignorante se condena: eso me pasa a mí, digo, me pasó y no me volverá a pasar . . . Pero cuando yo salga de aquí, será otra cosa. (p. 220)

and who knows how many more people had fallen, will be falling, will be detained to rot in jail for my fault. To be a revolutionary is not only being a man with balls. You have to have a head that knows right from wrong. He who sins out of ignorance, is condemned to ignorance: that happens to me, I mean, it happened to me and its not going to happen again . . . But when I get out of here, it will be another thing.

As he projects a future that ironically does not exist, because he wanders hopelessly at the end of the novel, Caimacán reflects on tragic mistakes and incongruities between theory and practice. Belatedly, he realizes that a revolution is more than an individual, outward demonstration of masculinity; instead it has to be a collective act on the part of the masses to throw off the oppressors. But in the Chocó, people have been conditioned to accept their lot rather than to strive for revolutionary change.

The conservative takeover in Bogotá leads to a similar reaction throughout the country. Pedro José, the initial protagonist, is also affected:

Lo único que le faltó a Pedro José fue salir amarrado de Tadó. El cura parroco y los gamonales conservadores lo acusaron de ateo, de inducir a los alumnos por el camino del mal. (p. 176)

The only thing left for Pedro José was to leave defeated from Tadó. The parish priest and the conservative landowners accused him of being an atheist, of leading the students down the path of evil.

It appears that all of Pedro's good fortune has turned to nothing as he contemplates the future:

Todo lo hecho por escapar del barro, su más grande deseo—ahorrarse unos centavos para ir a la ciudad y estudiar—, todo lo veía Pedro José, aquí a sus pies, reducido a cenizas. (p. 178)

Everything done to escape from the dirt, his greatest desire—to save a few coins to go to the city and study—Pedro José saw it all, here at his feet, reduced to ashes.

Later, he is given a job in Istmina as a schoolteacher. This does not bode well for the future since, if history repeats itself, Pedro José will always be subjected to the political whims of those who rule the country.

Caimacán, on the other hand, is willing to convert his ideals concerning injustice and repression into direct action. When Isacito Rentería, a local folk hero, is wounded by the police and taken into custody, Caimacán and Juan Sabino, his brother, lead the armed assault on the garrison. In the ensuing losing battle, Juan Sabino is killed and Caimacán is forced to go into hiding. As an official *bandolero*, Caimacán laments not for himself but for the victims of violence and for Colombia. He evokes a *copla* he heard in Cértegui that sums up his own plight as well as that of many others:

> Qué desgracia la del pobre:
> Con hambre y sin qué comé,
> Tiene la madre muelta,
> Y de palto la mujé;
> Loj muchachito llorando:
> "Papa yo quiero comé,"
> Er comisario en la puelta:
> "Seño: vengo por ujté." (p. 217)

> What a disgrace the plight of the poor man
> Hungry and with nothing to eat

His mother is dead
His woman is giving birth;
The children crying
"Daddy I want to eat,"
The sheriff in the door:
"Mister: I've come for you."

This popular song is testimony to the poverty, hunger, despair, and oppression that are constants in the lives of the majority of the Chocó population. Although the ending of *The Jungle and the Rain* is ambivalent, with Caimacán faced with extinction, the message is clear. There is the need for a revolution, but it will not be achieved by wide-eyed slogan-bearers or misdirected revolutionaries.

To what extent, then, does *The Jungle and the Rain* convey a certain ideology to the reader? Regarding literary production and ideology, Terry Eagleton offers some comments that are pertinent to this discussion:

Literary works are not mysteriously inspired, or explicable simply in terms of their author's psychology. They are forms of perceptions, particular ways of seeing the world; and as such they have a relation to that dominant way of seeing the world which is the "social mentality" or ideology of an age. That ideology, in turn, is the product of the concrete social relations into which men enter at a particular time and place; it is the way those class-relations are experienced, legitimized and perpetuated.[13]

The Jungle and the Rain, as is the case with most Afro-Colombian fiction, is an attempt to break with the dominant ideology. Through its presentation of character, theme, and world view, the novel reveals a discontent with current oppressive societal structures. Politics and economics are prime motivating factors. The internal struggle between liberals and conservatives provides the backdrop for a fictional presentation of human misery and suffering. Yet it does not mask the incapacity of individuals in the Chocó to earn a decent living due to economic impotence.

Certainly *The Jungle and the Rain* was not "mysteriously inspired." Yet it does represent a way of perceiving the concrete social relations in Colombia from 1930 to 1950. Palacios's perspective is that of the underdog, and he shows how the underdog's relations with the rulers are experienced, legitimized, and perpetuated. The work embodies a social mentality that cries out for changes that will never occur.

At the beginning of this discussion reference was made to the review of *The Jungle and the Rain* that appeared in *Cromos*. The reviewer described the novel as a series of notes that are an external scheme for a book Palacios did not write. True, *The Jungle and the Rain* rambles as the author seeks to capture the experiences of a cross section of characters in a number of settings. What maintains the novel's internal coherence are images and motifs generated from the cultural milieu. Most of these are associated with suffering and violence, such as the impact of the Chocó Pacífico and the events of 9 April 1948, the date on which "La Violencia" officially began.

Palacios's protagonists, nevertheless, are presented with aspects of their culture intact. The popular idiom of the Chocó, the oral tradition, and a sense of community are sustaining forces in the face of adversity in both *The Stars Are Black* and *The Jungle and the Rain*. The manner in which the majority of Chocoans speak is in direct contrast to the official language of the rulers; this is evident in the last, fatal *copla* recalled by Caimacán. Rentería, poet, teller of tales, and conserver of the oral tradition, resists domination both culturally and physically, but nonetheless ends up in jail. The community, however, will survive, because history has taught its members to have faith only in themselves.

In *The Jungle and the Rain*, the relationship between the novel and Colombian social and historical reality is not merely one of reflected content but also involves an interplay of forms. That is to say, the manner in which the formal devices of the novel—language, plot, character, setting, point of view—transform and supplement the interpretation of Chocoan culture is at the heart of Palacios's work. The effective fusion of popular and official language to accentuate social differences, the positive emphasis on folk culture, as well as a plot structure arranged to encompass the multifaceted nature of the Chocó are characteristics of *The Jungle and the Rain* that are important to an understanding of the novel as literature and as ideology.

The Jungle and the Rain is filled with contradictions and ambiguities. The title's metaphor suggests a process of darkness and purification, of despair and enlightenment. The characters are caught up in these inconsistencies, which permeate the society from bottom to top. Ironically, from Palacios's point of view, neither justice nor redemption will be a factor in their lives. That is because struggle is at an individual level of feeling, valuing, perceiving, and believing rather than at a higher plane of confrontation and awareness of why the Chocó is as it is and of how to effect meaningful social change.

In both *The Stars Are Black* and *The Jungle and the Rain* survival in the present is more important than clinging to romantic notions of the past. For Israel and Pedro José, the main black protagonists, how to confront day-to-day reality is more pressing than conjuring up images of Africa. Nevertheless, the manner in which these protagonists relate to society, ethnic identity, cultural dualism, psychical liberation, and societal confrontation—key concepts in the black dispersion throughout the Americas—forms a crucial part of their perceptions and interactions.

These two novels by Arnoldo Palacios are typical of the literature written by Afro-Colombians. In both *The Stars Are Black* and *The Jungle and the Rain* there is a fusion of form and content, of style and technique to capture in literature some of the experiences of the Chocoan population. Published almost a decade apart and with different aims, these novels nonetheless are quite similar. They mine the cultural intertext of the impoverished Chocó to reveal profound insight into the human condition. In so doing, these two novels capture a great deal of *la especificidad americana*. Palacios is not concerned with remnants of African culture in Colombia. But by dwelling on blacks, he clearly demonstrates that they are victims of the centuries of neglect that characterize the plight of the majority of Colombians.

3. The Literary Synthesizer

Carlos Arturo Truque

Carlos Arturo Truque is the author of two volumes of short stories: *Hailstorm and Other Stories* (1953) and the posthumous *The Day Summer Ended and Other Stories* (1973; Truque died 8 January 1970). Outside his native Colombia, where he was born 28 October 1927 in Condoto, in the Chocó region, not much attention has been paid to the literary contributions of Truque. In fact, he is not even mentioned—nor is any other Afro-Colombian writer—in a recent study, *The Latin American Short Story: A Critical History*, which contains chapters on the development of the Spanish-American short story by Naomi Lindstrom, John S. Brushwood, and George McMurray.[1]

Truque is not referred to either in an earlier, highly acclaimed collection of critical essays edited by Enrique Pupo Walker.[2] These omissions are not due to Truque's reputation as a short-story writer, since he has received numerous accolades in Colombia for his literary craft. Many of the writers discussed in these two books of criticism are both more obscure than Truque and of lesser literary quality. This exclusion reflects the historical lack of attention given black writers in Spanish America. Also, the Spanish study in particular demonstrates the tendency by critics to rehash old authors and themes and to dress them up in new literary jargon instead of offering new insights into the contributions of some of Spanish America's most interesting writers.

To his credit, Luis Leal in his *Historia del cuento hispanoamericano* (*History of the Spanish-American Short Story*) summarizes the short-story production of Carlos Arturo Truque:

Sus personajes son casi siempre proletarios o campesinos, y sus temas los problemas de esos hombres que luchan por mejorar sus pésimas condiciones de vida. No son los de Truque, sin embargo, cuentos de tesis, ya que su actitud es imparcial y solo deja que las acciones reflejen esos problemas sociales contra los que combate.[3]

His characters are almost always workers or rural people, and his themes the problems of those men who fight to better their abominable living conditions. Those of Truque are not, nevertheless, thesis stories, since his attitude is impartial and he lets actions reflect the social problems against which his protagonists battle.

Leal is one of the few literary historians who views Truque as a part of the long and rich *cuentista* traditions of Spanish America. He situates Truque in the same neorealist literary generation as Manuel Mejía Vallejo, a renowned Colombian novelist and short-story writer, because of their common affinity for protagonists who struggle against adversity to survive. In his creation of environment, character, and language, Truque also bears a strong literary resemblance to the late Juan Rulfo, one of Mexico's finest writers.

In Colombia, Truque is recognized as a master of the short story by enlightened critics, and his works have appeared in a dozen anthologies. Strangely, Truque is referred to by the novelist Gustavo Alvarez Gardeazábal as a "*chocoano* who wrote about the exciting legends of the rainiest and therefore the most isolated part of the country."[4] Perhaps Gardeazábal is confusing Truque with Arnoldo Palacios, because I am unaware of a body of work by Truque interpreting the circumstances Gardeazábal mentions.

In an insightful interview with J. M. Alvarez D'Orsonville conducted in 1960 for the radio program "Colombia Literaria," Truque made some profound statements regarding the short story as a genre and its development in Colombia. Responding to a question concerning his opinion of the genre, Truque stated:

In our country the short story has not developed as it seems to me it should have. So exacting a form demands certain qualities of observation, psychological sharpness, and a capacity for synthesis that not everyone possesses. The overwhelming inclination of our writers to poetry has meant that the story, the novel, and the essay, to say nothing of the theatre, have been badly neglected. In answer to the second part of the question, a story is brevity; it is the synthesis of a vital moment. A good short story writer knows how to give the necessary depth to the characters he is describing with a few strokes and sufficient intensity, in any episode, however simple or common it may be.[5]

One of the reasons for the dearth of good short-story writers in Colombia, according to Truque, is the tendency by Colombian authors to adorn their creations with a "certain poetic-symbolic splendor" that is counterproductive. He also states that Colombia does not have a short-story tradition because its writers' stories have "lacked vigorous and sustained quality."

In response to a question concerning the disdain of Colombian writers for native themes, Truque attributes this attitude to "a romantic longing for universality and also to the fact that they care too much for their own literary reputations." He continues:

There is no one in Colombia who dares to think differently from the editor of the periodical which publishes his articles. In this sense, the writer is merely a salaried employee of the great press, a peon who identifies politically with the property owners and is strictly faithful to what they demand of him. The writer in Colombia, a country of human rights and of civil law, does not have the freedom to forge a great national literature. For when he is not the beggarly appendage of a party, access to the media of communication is made impossible for him. How then can a writer make himself known to his people, especially in a country which does not have a well-directed publishing industry?[6]

These comments raise issues that are fundamental to most writers concerning audience, tradition, and publishing opportunities. Truque interprets his situation as being exacerbated due to the Colombian cultural milieu, which views the underdog as unimportant both socially and as a topic for literature. A great deal of the prose fiction of Afro-Colombians has not been well received, and the writers attribute this phenomenon to the themes that they treat and to the social attitudes of their country.

It is interesting to examine how Truque puts into practice the qualities and characteristics he attributes to a good short story.[7] These include not only "qualities of observation," "psychological sharpness," and "a capacity for synthesis" that the writer must possess, but also the author's ability to transform material into an "exhaustive description of a vital moment."

Many of these vital moments interpreted by Truque are plagued with violence, terror, alienation, and dehumanization. Rarely is there a positive moment in the interactions of his literary characters. Rather, most of them are so engrossed in the struggle to survive that they do not pause to think of the positive in their lives. Hunger is a recurring motif in Truque's works, just as it is such an integral part of the novels of Arnoldo Palacios. For both authors, the force of this instinctual drive causes men to react irrationally in their relations with others.

In Truque's short stories, the implied author is not as apparent as in the works of the other writers examined in this study. His narrative strategy is to present a set of literary circumstances and to let readers draw their own conclusions as to meaning without intrusion from the literary creator. The manner in which characters and circumstances are presented, however, leaves no doubt that Truque is at odds with Colombian society.

In initially placing Truque within the tradition of the Spanish-American short story, it is useful to cite George McMurray who, under the subheading "1950-1959: Protest and Universality," observes:

The most noteworthy writers of short fiction during the 1940's reveal a marked tendency toward universality, emphasizing metaphysical, literary and psychological themes. By contrast, the works of the 1950s convey a stronger awareness of the political and social problems plaguing much of Spanish America.[8]

These latter observations are certainly applicable to the stories of Carlos Arturo Truque that were published collectively as *Hailstorm and Other Stories* in 1953. Although Truque is demonstrably aware of Colombia's social and political problems, he does not, as Leal points out, allow this concern to result in thesis stories. Rather, his concern is for literary authenticity, a manner in which to convey *La especificidad latinoamericana*.

Most of Carlos Arturo Truque's short stories do not deal specifically with the Afro-Colombian situation. Rather, he assesses the plight of the rural and urban poor in general. This is in keeping with Truque's literary vocation, which went against the current of Colombian letters until late in his career. In an autobiographical piece, Truque remarks: "Para quienes quieren una forma artística, nutrida de las condiciones de vida de la gran masa del pueblo colombiano, el camino está vedado" (For those who want an artistic form nourished from the conditions of life of the great mass of Colombian people, the path is forbidden).[9] He goes on to state that at this early juncture of his career it was difficult for him to gain recognition because the literary elite in Colombia was more interested in escapism and European models than in works interpreting national reality.

In reacting to the commonly held assumption that the masses have no interest in literature, Truque asserts:

Y no quiere leer porque no comprende; porque no se ve reflejado en la obra; porque el pueblo, no teniendo cultura, sabe reconocerse y comprende, si alguien está bien intencionado respecto a él, los derroteros que se le señalan. No deben olvidar nuestros europeizantes que las épocas más floridas de la literatura universal han estado normadas por los pueblos y los escritores no han sido sino meros escribanos, artesanos por mejor decirlo, de la voluntad popular.[10]

And they do not wish to read because they cannot; because they do not see themselves reflected in the work; because the people, not having culture, knows how to recognize itself and understands, if someone is well intentioned toward them, the direction that they point out. Our europeanizers must not forget that the most flourishing periods of universal literature have been defined by the people and the writers have not been more than mere chroniclers, artisans to better state it, of the popular will.

It is safe to assume that most of Truque's stories will be high in human content, voicing consistent literary and personal ideals. The most effective way to approach his thematic variety is through a formalist examination of theme and technique.

Hailstorm and Other Stories

Both of Truque's published volumes interpret the Colombian milieu, rural and urban, from the perspective of the underdog, thus giving voice to those incapable of articulating their own circumstances. The epigraph to the first story in *Hailstorm and Other Stories* reads: "Even the she wolf has her lair: only the son of man does not have a rock on which to rest his head."[11] It is useful, first of all, to summarize each story, and then to view them within the larger context of the volume as a whole.

"Porque así era la gente" ("Because People Were This Way"), the first of nine selections, is a story of despair. It recounts a night in the life of an unnamed protagonist, an emigrant from Cali to Bogotá, and his attempt to come to grips with unemployment, poverty, hunger, and despair in an uncaring urban environment. He "entered," "kept busy," "saw," and "remained" are the images of permanency that describe his less than concrete situation. He enters a bar for warmth and companionship but at closing time is forced to take to the streets again.

Out of desperation, the protagonist deliberately breaks a store window and is arrested. From the perspective of a jail cell he observes:

Afuera quedaba la calle fría, inhumana, bestial, con su olor a aguardiente y prostitución, en cada esquina un policía empujando a otros hombres fuera de la vida. El dormiría y quizá mañana le dieran hasta de comer 'porque así era la gente . . . .' (p. 14)

Outside remained the cold street, inhumane, bestial, with its odor of liquor and prostitution, on each corner a policeman pushing other men out of life. He would sleep and perhaps tomorrow they would even give him something to eat "because that's the way the people were . . . ."

This brief, intense sketch captures the desperation of the

downtrodden, the sentiment of hopelessness so prevalent among the urban dispossessed.

"Las gafas oscuras" ("The Dark Sunglasses"), the second story, is built around the irony of a pickpocket who is watched by a blind man. Although it is written with not quite the dramatic force of the preceding selection, in this story Truque nevertheless captures the intensity of the moment in the actions of a pickpocket who is about to rob a fellow passenger. The pickpocket hesitates, ironically, because he is under the vigilant scrutiny of a blind man, thereby losing his prey.

"Martín encuentra dos razones" ("Martín Finds Two Reasons"), just as the majority of Truque's stories, is also structured around a single incident. Martín, an employee, goes with his boss to a brothel on Christmas Eve with the hope that this show of camaraderie will result in a pay raise. There, Martín encounters Marta, who represents his erotic fantasies and with whom he reluctantly spends the night. At home the next morning he is greeted by Josefa, his wife, and the boring circumstances of their existence. Martín observes:

Allí estaban la butaca, el radio, el sofá, las lámparas, el reloj de péndulo. Cada cosa tenía la misma expresión que tenía cuando fueron adqueridas. Tal parecía que se hubieran adaptado mutuamente. (p. 29)

There were the easy chair, the radio, the sofa, the lamps, the grandfather clock. Each thing had the same expression they had when they were first purchased. So much so that it seemed they had adjusted mutually.

In spite of the monotony of the physical surroundings, Martín's wife does seem to have changed: "Por primera vez se percató de que ésta había envejecido" (For the first time he noticed that she had aged; p. 29). Josefa cannot compete with the tender, young Marta, who represents youth and an epoch that cannot be recaptured. But because Martín is a responsible individual, he does not keep his promise to return to the prostitute. Instead, he stores her in his memory and, for the sake of his two children, stays at home.

"La noche de San Silvestre" ("The Night of San Silvestre") is a tragic story depicting the plight of the poor in their struggle for survival. The plot contrasts the festive atmosphere of New Year's Eve with the depressing circumstances of a couple whose son is dying of an undiagnosed illness. The metaphoric city comes to life in its most ironic dimension as it seems to be mocking the desperate father:

Recorrió la ciudad afiebrada, en su delirio del final del año, estremecida de pólvora de chisporroteos y música. La ciudad con la gente alocada, riendo y gritando porque sí, sin motivo alguno para estar feliz. Tal parecía que una mano siniestra y burlona, para su diversión les hubiera extendida las jetas y les hubiera marcado la mancha blanca de la risa, a la fuerza, en un acto físico sin correspondencia anímica alguna. Pasaba un borracho y se reía; pasaba un mendigo, con sus harapos, y reía, también sin saber que se estaba riendo de sí mismo. (p. 34)

He crisscrossed the feverish city, in its end-of-the-year-delirium, rendered with the dust of sparkles and music. The city with its crazy people laughing and shouting in spite of it all, without any motive for being happy. It seemed as though a sinister and joking hand, for its entertainment, had extended its snout to them and had marked the white stain of a smile, with force, in a physical act without any psychic correspondence. A drunk passed by and laughed; a beggar passed in rags, and laughed, also without knowing that he was laughing at himself.

The false posture assumed by the city on this festive occasion does not mask human suffering. The irony of the negative position of these underdogs is underscored by metaphors of happiness. "To laugh" and its different variations are indicative of this dilemma: "laughing," "smile," "laughed." Caught up in this euphoric environment, most people tend to forget their troubles, but not the father whose son is dying. The false smiles trigger in his imagination the image of an uncaring, smiling physician who refuses to leave a party to tend to the dying son. This story captures, masterfully, another moment of human anguish in an insensitive urban environment.

"La muerte tuvo cara y sello" ("Death Had a Face and Seal") is a tale of betrayal and revenge within a triangular affair between a wife, her husband, and her lover. Told from the perspective of Pepe, the husband, at the wake of Teresa, the wife, the plot details how Pepe trapped Teresa in a compromising situation with their friend Suárez and forced them to suffer the consequences.

During the brief confrontation in Suárez's apartment, Pepe makes Suárez pay Teresa for her favors with a coin. Pepe subsequently uses this memento to humble and manipulate them publicly and privately, and he is convinced that the coin leads to her demise. When Pepe is asked for the death certificate, the following occurs:

Pero, ante la sorpresa de los concurrentes, depositó en la mano que se alargó a recibirlo, la moneda, en lugar del papelito arrugado en donde el médico había garrapateado las causas de la muerte de Teresa. (p. 52)

But, before the surprised look of the audience, he deposited in the hand which reached out to receive it, the coin, instead of the little wrinkled piece of paper on which the doctor had scribbled the causes of Teresa's death.

"Granizada" ("Hailstorm"), the title story of this volume, assesses a rural situation of humans against the elements. As the story opens, a family is facing an impending hailstorm that threatens to destroy its crops and its livelihood. Eulalia, the mother, attempts to use celestial powers to avoid disaster. She is faithful and believes that her family will be spared through a miracle. Her faith is in stark contrast to the attitude of her husband, who is concerned with practical, worldly matters and equates God with the bank because they both control the destiny of *campesinos*.

For a moment, it seems as if prayers have been answered, but the crops are destroyed. Realizing that they are at the mercy of the elements, the father reacts with a final gesture of impotence by destroying the religious icons in anger. In a final anguished scene, father and son admit defeat:

> —¡Mijo!—gruñó el padre—. ¡Mijo! . . . Nos tragó la diabla . . . .
> El mozo corrió hacia él y lo tomó del brazo, no sin cierta vacilación:
> —Camine apá, camine. Esto ya se perdió . . . Fíjese que ni la Virgen . . . Ni ansiquiera ella quiso ser güena con nosotros . . . (p. 64)

> "My son!" grumbled the father. "My son! . . . the devil swallowed us up . . ."
> The boy ran toward him and took him by the arm, not without some hesitation:
> "Come on Papa, come on. That's already lost . . . look not even the Virgin . . . Not even she wanted to be good to us . . ."

At this moment of existential torment, characters are presented as at the mercy of both the human and the natural orders.

"Sangre en el llano" ("Blood on the Plains") is an account of death, violence, and revenge among the *llaneros*. An environment of sterility and silence prefigures the impending doom and carnage: "La sequía puso su sonrisa de bilis a los pastizales desenrizados, en la llanura herida por las pezuñas de la vacada" (The drought put its smile of bile on the uprooted pastures, in the grassland wounded by the hoofs of the herd; p. 66). In this instance, nature is humanized in a negative sense, and it anticipates reciprocal violent acts by humans.

Within the harsh imagery of the countryside, a drama of vengeance is being acted out. A group of men led by Luis Uruquijo is preparing to attack an enemy band of cattle drivers who in the past had violated Uruquijo and his family. He remembers:

Amarrado al horcón había visto cómo saciaron su apetito de bestias sobre las carnes desgarradas de la mujer que amaba. ¡Cómo le había dolido la respiración jadeante, cortada de lujurias, los besos de la cópula asquerosa, chasqueantes como latigazos! . . . ¡Tener que soportar el expresivo suplicar de sus ojos, semejantes a los de los cristos agónicos de la iglesia pueblerina! (p. 69)

Tied up to the stake, he had seen how they satisfied their bestial appetites upon the torn flesh of the woman he loved. How it had pained him, the heavy breathing, proportioned with lust, the kisses of the loathsome copulation, cracking like whip lashes! To have to bear the expressive pleading of her eyes, similar to those of suffering Christs in the village church.

Uruquijo retains this image of degradation as he prepares to exact justice at the expense of the violators. The sadistic practice of making him watch while his wife is violated emphasizes the dehumanizing nature of the violent union as revealed in "bestial appetites," "torn flesh," "loathsome copulation." Uruquijo gets even in ritualistic fashion: "El cuchillo certero ascendía encendido por el sol. El primer golpe fue como el rasgarse de una tela gruesa" (The well-aimed knife rose ignited by the sun. The first blow was like the ripping of a coarse cloth; pp. 70–71). Once vengeance/justice has been achieved, the dramatic tension eases and life returns to normal on the plains.

"La fuga" ("Flight") is the story of a tormented soul secluded in madness after the death of his family. It describes an attempt, on the part of the adult protagonist, to escape to the refuge of childhood in order to avoid the pressures of day-to-day life. The technical device of interior monologue captures the thoughts, reactions, and perceptions of the witness/protagonist.

"Lo triste de vivir así" ("The Sadness of Living This Way") is a narrative of failure in marriage and the lonely consequences of being unemployed. The story is told in first person from the perspective of self-denigration: "Soy una calamnidad. Realmente no sirvo para nada. Razón de sobra tiene mi mujer cuando me lo grita" (I am a calamity. Really I'm not worth anything. My wife has more than enough justification when she shouts at me; p. 78). Self-pity, the state into which the narrator has lapsed, is not a sufficient escape mechanism. His early romantic notions of marriage have disintegrated into the current situation, in which "vivimos como perros y gatos, disgustando por detalles, por insignificancias" (we live like dogs and cats falling out over details, over nothing; p. 80).

The reader learns that the narrator has reached his current state because of life's chance adversities. If possible, he would ask the Colombian president:

¿Qué destino reserva para mis hijos? Yo mismo respondería. Ella, la pequeña, llegará a ser una buena vagabunda y él, Antonio, un ratero. No alcanzo a ver más. (p. 83)

What future is in store for my children? I myself would respond. She, the little one, will become a good tramp and he, Antonio, a thief. I can't see anything more.

The narrator is successfully projecting sentiments of frustration and insecurity upon the next generation and his wife in order to compensate for his own perceived inadequacies. Ironically, there is no future hope for them, as is the case for many of Truque's protagonists.

"Because the People Were This Way," "Martin Finds Two Reasons," "The Night of San Silvestre," and "The Sadness of Living This Way" are the best presentations in this volume of the urban environment. The city exemplifies a situation of degradation, hunger, and prostitution—prostitution not in its superficial dimension, but as a last resort for survival. The city, which has always been a safety valve for the rural poor, becomes a metaphor for hopelessness and despair, a presence that mock its victims.

"Hailstorm" and "Blood on the Plain" present rural characters at the mercy of the elements and human passions. In the first story the unanswered question seems to be, if God is not on our side, then who is? Life's accidents and social determinism become crucial factors in deciding individual destinies. The cycles of violence and revenge only provide momentary satisfaction that still leaves the individual with the problems of the present.

What is presented in *Hailstorm and Other Stories* are exhaustive descriptions of a vital moment in the lives of the protagonists. The reader, when confronted with a crucial moment in life, reacts to how the narrator structures his episode around this moment. The author is very perceptive in his synthesis of the situation and how it affects the protagonist, thereby demonstrating the ability to incorporate minute details and descriptions. Both internal processes and the surface of events are incorporated into a coherent presentation of environment. Themes of violence and alienation reinforce images of dehumanization that unify the collective experience of the downtrodden in Colombia.

Truque mines both the uncaring urban environment and the harsh rural countryside in his presentations. In both locales the downtrodden, the underdogs, do not overcome; instead they find themselves at the mercy of circumstances beyond their control. Whether the destitute urban protagonist of "Because the People Were This Way" or the victims in "Hailstorm," the poor reach center stage in this first volume by Carlos Arturo Truque. In this regard the writer achieved his longed-for status as "craftsman of the popular will."

Of the themes shared with other writers in this study, violence and alienation are the most characteristic of Truque's work. The estrangement from self, others, and society that the protagonists experience in "Because the People Were This Way" is placed in a different context, but with similar results, in "Hailstorm." The horizontal and individual violence of "Blood on the Plain" manifests the sentiments in the countryside that are suppressed in the urban environment of "The Night of San Silvestre."

There is not a positive story in this collection. While there is no overt "social" criticism, Truque's message is clear. In order to alleviate the hunger, suffering, and disjointed existence of the Colombian poor, some fundamental changes have to be made in the society as a whole.

The Day Summer Ended and Other Stories

The Day Summer Ended and Other Stories consists of fourteen stories. Half of them are from the previous volume, while seven are new in book form. These seven are: "The Day Summer Ended," "Sonatina para dos tambores"

("Sonata for Two Drums"), "El encuentro" ("The Encounter"), "Fucú," "La diana" ("Reveille"), "El misterio" ("The Mystery"), and "Dos hombres" ("Two Men"). In this second volume, Truque continues to write about themes common to his earlier works.

Just as *Hailstorm and Other Stories* fit within the tradition of short-story writing in Spanish America in the 1950s as outlined by George McMurray, so this book falls within the critical framework outlined by McMurray for the 1960s in his discussion of "Innovative Forms and the Boom":

> During the 1960s the short story as a genre continued the major trends of the preceding decade, reflecting the political realities as well as the philosophical and esthetic preoccupations of a wide variety of writers. Although during the decade of the much-touted Boom the novel tended to overshadow short fiction, the short story of the 1960s reached heights of quality and originality that remained unsurpassed to the present.[12]

Truque's short stories written during this period reflect the political, philosophical, and aesthetic concerns prevalent throughout Latin America. His ability to combine form and content greatly enhances his mastery of the art of story telling.

"The Day Summer Ended" is Truque's most anthologized short story. Its popularity is due to a fusion of form and content that is symbolic of human experience and perseverance. This story has an archetypal underpinning that reinforces a transition from death to life. In an ironic literary reversal of seasons, summer is presented as the epoch of sterility and barrenness while the onset of winter promises rain and the restoration of life to the crops.

Don Pedro, from whose perspective the narrative is presented, waits, both for the change of seasons and for word of his brother José, who left when he could no longer tolerate the battle for survival in an unyielding environment. A message arrives in the person of María Mercedes, José's woman, who informs Don Pedro of José's death. María symbolizes both hope and fertility. In her quest for water in which to bathe, she becomes a very erotic presence.

From the moment of María's arrival, Pedro's thoughts are on her:

pero ahora no lo atrajo más el campo a medio arar, ni los surcos amarillentos, ni la yerba quemada, sino ella, la hembra, y tembló por dentro, porque pensaba en cómo sería el deslizar una mano lentamente por sus flancos, su vientre, y luego dejarla ir hacia abajo, en una incursión franca y atrevida.[13]

but now the half-plowed field did not attract him, nor did the yellow furrows, nor the burned grass, but her, the woman, and he trembled within, because he thought about how it would be to slide his hand slowly across her flanks, her stomach, and then let it go below in a frank and daring incursion.

Here, the association between cultivating the soil and copulation is made for the first time in the story. Other images of sowing seeds and fertilization are interwoven into the narrative structure as the infertility of the soil is contrasted to the robustness of María. The opposition established between her and the soil is reflected in the ambivalence of Pedro toward her, "cuyas formas generosas le traín y lo repelían simultaneamente" (whose generous forms attracted him and repelled him at the same time; p. 13).

María represents life in a dying environment. At one point Pedro identifies her with water: "Ella con el agua y yo con ella, carajo" (She with the water and me with her, damn; p. 19), intensifying the ironic nature of the story to the point of projecting his sexual fantasies on similar acts by their horses:

Por fin, en una de tantas vueltas, el caballo alcanzó la yegua, le puso los remos en los cuartos traseros y luego él vio el impulso del caballo, con un pequeño salto hacia adelante, para quedar luego quietos caballo y yegua, relinchando de vez en cuando. (p. 25)

Finally, in one of many turns, the stallion reached the mare, he put his legs on her hindquarters and then he saw the force of the horse, with a little jump forward, to remain calm, then stallion and mare, neighing from time to time.

"The Day Summer Ended" culminates in a final scene of sexual integration as the rain comes:

> La mujer estaba en un prado, desnuda, revolcándose, ayudándose con las manos para que el agua la mojara por completo.
> El la vio como era: gorda, llenita, de piernas gruesas. Al verlo parado, con el saco a la espalda, aguantando a pie firme la lluvia, rió infantilmente. Y él se dio vuelta y emprendió carrera, para seguir regando su maíz, con el alma alegre por todo: porque José María se había ido; porque había mandado la mujer; porque ella estaba ahora desnuda en el campo; porque él estaba sembrando bajo el aguacero que ella había traído para bañarse y para acabar, en esa forma, el largo e impiadoso VERANO. (p. 27)

> The woman was in a meadow, naked, turning around, helping herself with her hands so that the water would wet her completely.
> He saw her as she was: stout, full-figured, with thick legs. Upon seeing him stopped there, with the coat on his back, she laughed childishly. And he turned and began to walk away, to continue planting his corn, with his soul happy about everything: because José María had gone away; because he had sent the woman; because she was now naked in the field; because he was planting beneath the rainshower that she had brought to bathe herself and to finish, in that way, the long and cruel SUMMER.

María is consistently described with images of plenty—"gorda," "llenita"—and in Pedro's mind is the cause of all his good fortune. Here the disparate elements associated with fertility and sex are intertwined, as the narrative suggests that Pedro will finish sowing his grain seeds and join María for a rainy sexual initiation of the winter season. This is one of the few positive stories among Truque's published works.

Several key universal symbols are integral to the story's internal coherence. Archetypally, according to Wilfred Guerin, water represents "the mystery of creation; birth-death-resurrection; purification and redemption; fertility and growth." The Archetypal Woman, in this case the Earth Mother represented by María, "is associated with birth, warmth, protection, fertility, growth and abundance." The desert symbolizes "spiritual aridity; death; nihilism or hopelessness."[14] "The Day Summer Ended" begins with a concrete situation of hopelessness but ends on a note of hope. Through a fusion of imagery and narrative technique, the story transcends the local situation to assume universal significance. It is therefore reflective of the quality and originality described by McMurray at the beginning of this chapter.

It is also interesting to view how Truque handles an Afro-Colombian theme given the fact that he does not often distinguish between blacks and the poor in that country. Truque's only story treating ethnicity is "Sonata for Two Drums," which is built on contrasts—between past and present, fantasy and reality. The drums referred to in the title are both the labored breathing of Damiana on her deathbed and the lively activities associated with the feast of Santa Barbara in the river town of Timbiquí. Told from the perspective of Santiago, Damiana's husband, this is a tale of death, sexual frustration, and compassion in the context of Afro-Colombian culture.

On the one hand Santiago agonizes with Damiana: "le dolía el aire y lo cogía por la nariz para que le saliera otra vez por los fuelles con un sonido de 'conuno' retemplado" (the air pained her, and he grabbed her by the nose so that again it left through her bellows with the sound of a tempered drum; p. 28). Santiago, at the same time, reminisces about happier times associated with the carnival and Guillermina, "una negra reidora que poco a poco se le iba volviendo 'el tormento de sus tormentos'; y que aunque no le había dado un besito, lo traía más alzado que una nube y más golpeado que tambor de Día de Reyes" (a smiling black woman who little by little went stirring up "the torment of his torments"; and even though she had not even given him a kiss, it brought him more height than a cloud and more action than a drum on Three Kings Day; p. 31). Physically, Santiago is faced with the imminent death of his wife, while mentally he conjures up forbidden images that only serve to torment him further.

The level of Santiago's anxiety increases in proportion to the decline of Damiana's health, resulting in a powerful poetic expression of death:

El allí dándose su gusto, tirando de los compases como de una cuerda, diablo de negro mandinga, con la boca como brasa "del patacoré" "que se va a cae," se iba sintiendo mejor. Y allá en la tiniebla, la Damiana con su aire y sus pulmones que no daban más, sorbiendo espeso, sacándoles un último lance a las manos para sus dos conunos flácidos, que apenas vibraron un postrer compás antes de quedarse en paz, priváditos. Solo simples cueros, sin aire posible ni dolor probable. (p. 39)

Him over there having his fun, whirling with the beat as if on a string, devil of a black *mandinga*, with a mouth like a coal from the *patacoré* (fiery dance), it's going to happen, he was feeling better. And there in the darkness, Damiana with her air and her lungs that gave no more, breathing deeply, taking from them a last chance for the hands for her two weak drums, that hardly vibrated a last beat before remaining in peace, private. Only plain skins without possible air or probable pain.

This mixture of the festive and the tragic underscores the ironic basis of "Sonata for Two Drums," a situation that is defined by Santiago within the tradition of popular culture that he knows best.

In an article concerning the African influence on music and dance in Latin America, Isabel Aretz remarks: "In Colombia the Cumbia, the Mapale, the Bullerenque, and the Currulao all equally retain typical musical characteristics, in addition to their names, which are not Hispanic." The Currulao, the dance that frames "Sonata for Two Drums," is described by Aretz in the following manner:

El currulao del litoral Pacífico se tocó con marimbas, dos cununos o tambores cónicos de un solo parche, dos bombos (macho y hembra) y los guasas o idiofonos tubulares de sacudimiento. El coro, a cargo generalmente de las mujeres, se desarrolló utilizando versos reiterados, estribillos y fonemas, sujetándose al proceso rítmico y dejando que la melodía del canto se diluya sin relieve vocal.[15]

The Currulao of the Pacific Coast is played with marimbas, two *cununos* or conical-shaped drums with one drumhead, two *bombos* (male and female drums), and the *guasas* or tubular instruments for shaking. The chorus, generally the charge of the women, is developed using repeated verses, refrains, and phonemes, subjecting itself to the rhythmic process and letting the melody of the song dilute without vocal relief.

Santiago, the protagonist, at the same time that he is witnessing the physical decline of his wife, Damiana, is vicariously reliving past sensual encounters with other women. The activities transpire around a festival for the patron saint of the town of Santa Barbara de Timbiquí. Santa Barbara is known locally as "the patron against thunder" and in the Afro-Hispanic Catholic pantheon is a syncretized version of the Yoruba god Changó, who is venerated in the Americas as the God of war, fecundity, and dance. In "Sonata for Two Drums," then, Truque has gone beyond the rhetorical level to present a "literature of African survival" that attempts to treat African elements in Colombian society without connecting them directly to Africa.

Otherwise, Truque's stories contain little of the African literary presence outlined by Brathwaite in my Introduction. When it is present, Africa is either on the "rhetorical" plane or a manifestation of "literature of African survival" as seen in "Sonata for Two Drums." Truque is what Richard Jackson would label "a realistically committed black author who writes from within" and, in theme and technique, represents literary Americanism/Colombianism at its very best, as demonstrated in the story just discussed.

"The Encounter" studies the effects of a factory on life in a *barriada*. It explores internal family strife and some of the problems associated with unionization. The story also examines individual commitment to an ideal. Alonso, the main protagonist, is on strike for better wages and working conditions. María, his wife, constantly reminds him that a little bit of something is more than a whole lot of nothing. She encourages him to return to work but at the same time realizes that her husband's actions are justified. The dichotomy in "The Encounter" is between the economic security the factory could provide and the abject poverty in which the workers live and from which they wish to break.

"Fucú" is a tale of superstition and pride. Retrospectively, the narrative assesses the decisions of Emiliano Torreblanca, an ex-ship's captain who goes often to the seashore to observe the decaying remains of his boat, *La Marianita*. Early in life Emiliano had fallen in love with a woman named Mariana and wished to take her to sea with him. This violated the belief commonly held by his crew that "¡Barco que lleva mujer, le cae fucú!" (A ship that carries a woman will be befallen by *fucú*; p. 56). Torreblanca and *La Marianita* are abandoned by the crew, and he is unable to recruit more sailors; but he refuses to sell his boat. He fantasizes about being a captain while the real-life relationship with Mariana deteriorates. She abandons him to his stubbornness and his memories:

Emiliano Torreblanca ya no era capitán de la otra Mariana. Había perdido el mar de la ternura como antes perdiera el otro. Por esta razón viene a ver la otra "Marianita," volcada en el lodo; ésta no saldrá para ningún puerto. La ata el facú, maldición de mujer sobre los hierros carcomidos. (p. 60)

Emiliano Torreblanca was now not captain of the other Mariana. He had lost the sea of tenderness as before he had lost the other. For this reason he comes to see the other "Marianita," wallowing in the mud; this one will not leave for any port. She is tied by *facú*, curse of a woman upon those rusting hulls.

Torreblanca still waits and watches.

"Reveille" is a story of violence, brutality, and machismo set during the one-thousand-days war during the early epoch of "La Violencia" in Colombia at the turn of the century. It recounts the physical and mental ordeal of Matías Gamboa, a prisoner, at the hands of his old enemy, Colonel Ruperto García. Early in life, they had an altercation involving manhood and the fact that Marcela, Matías's wife, had given birth to a daughter instead of a son. García insults Matías: "—Para zamparle un macho a Marcela se necesita un hombre . . . —y se río con su risa vulgar, abierta como piernas de prostituta" ("To give a male child to Marcela a man is necessary . . ." and he laughed with his vulgar laugh, open like the legs of a prostitute; p. 65). Since he cannot father a son, Matías is obviously not a real man.

This attitude is exacerbated when García returns to the

town as leader of the occupying forces, imprisons Matías, and sentences him to "reveille" treatment, which involves being beaten to the tune of a drum-and-bugle corps. As he awaits his fate, Matías thinks of his wife, who is again pregnant, and of the possibility that this child might be a son. At the same time, he is concerned with his own macho image and determined not to demonstrate weakness during the punishment. He subsequently fuses the masculine images in his mind during the beating:

Y le pareció que al dirigir la vista al frente, el alba se le cerraba, e imaginó que se la estaba sorbiendo por los ojos, de afuera hacia adentro. Escuchó, como entre quien duerme y no duerme, una voz diciendo:
—Es un hombre, carajo, es un hombre . . .
Y él, sin saber por qué se acordó una vez más de Marcela y las varas y las rosas rojas, todo en uno, confundido; y recordó eso de ella en el monte y su manera de ser imperativa, mientras el mundo se le iba diluyendo en una masa de sombra densa. Y se escuchó con voz desasida, sola y vaga, diciendo:
—Sabía que iba a ser un hombre . . . (p. 71)

And it seemed to him that on directing his glance forward, the dawn closed in on him, and he imagined that he was absorbing it through his eyes, from outside to within. He listened, like one who is between sleep and wakefulness, to a voice saying:
"It's a man, damn, it's a man . . . —And he, without knowing why, remembered one more time about Marcela and the weeds and the red roses, all in one, confused; and he remembered about her in the mountains and her manner of being imperative, while the world was slipping away from him in a mass of dense shadow. And he listened with a distant voice, alone and vague, saying:
"I knew it was going to be a man . . ."

Whether "it is a man" describes the victim or his son is not clear. Matías is oblivious to his physical suffering, but he has resolved questions concerning his masculinity and is therefore willing to confront the ultimate obstacle of death.

"Two Men" is a story of poverty and desperation whose action takes place during several intense hours in the lives of Pedro Vengoechea and Jorge Beltrán, whose greatest need is food. Bitterness is an image that dominates the text from the taste of the first drops of seawater on Pedro's lips to the bitter fruit they harvest in the form of apples stolen from aboard ship, an action that results in their incarceration. The story's central metaphor is summarized by Jorge in reaction to Pedro's description of the water: "—Una salmuera, amigo,— agregó pausadamente—como nuestras vidas" ("a brine, friend," he added measuredly, "like our lives"; p. 102). In both "Because the People Were This Way" from the previous volume and "Two Men," the hunger/jail metaphors are constructed to emphasize a situation of despair in which men are stripped of their dignity in order to survive.

Two basic ironies undergird the story. The first occurs when Pedro asks Jorge his name and the latter answers, "de Santander, de donde son los machos" (from Santander, where the men come from; p. 102) To Pedro, origins and physical prowess are not as important as hunger. The other ironic situation involves imports and exports and is developed as the two men watch the ship offload and Pedro remarks that he once planted coffee:

—¿Si? . . . Pues ya sabes para dónde viene lo que sembras. Damos café y nos devuelven automóviles de lujo. Vos lo sembraste pero otro que no conoces, te pisará con el carro que compró con tu sudor . . . Es la vida. (p. 104)

"Yes? . . . Well you already know where what you sow goes. We give coffee and they return us luxury automobiles. You sowed it but another that you don't know will run over you with the car that you bought with your sweat . . . That's life."

Although Pedro and Jorge are misfits, socially declassed, they demonstrate a keen awareness of how the class system functions and the impact of the rift between rich and poor in Colombia. Natural resources are exploited to the fullest to support an alien life-style while many people starve.

"The Mystery" has a religious theme and recounts the anguish experienced by the parish priest of Majagual, Fray Mario de la Concepción. Jewels have been stolen from a necklace that adorns the Virgin and replaced by fake glass.

The mystery surrounds who the culprit is and why. The problem is resolved on a fantastic note as the jewels are returned in plain view of most of the townspeople:

Desde la puerta de entrada, vio avanzar una figura borrosa, no identificada, no sabía si por las lágrimas que tenía como telerañas en las pupilas o porque la figura carecía de rostro. No solamente él la vio. La vieron todos y todos vieron, asimismo, lo que portaba en sus manos. El comisario quiso abalanzarse sobre ella, pero se sintió clavado en el sitio, y el resto de la muchedumbre, lo mismo. (pp. 98–99)

From the entrance door he saw advancing a fuzzy, unidentified figure, he did not know if because of the tears that he had like spiderwebs in his pupils or because the figure lacked a face. He was not the only one that saw it. They all saw it, and they all saw, likewise, what it carried in its hands. The commissioner wanted to pounce upon her, but he felt nailed to his seat, and the rest of the crowd, the same.

This incident remains in the realm of the inexplicable, but the anonymous witness-narrator pretends to have the answer. He or she believes the one-legged beggar is the culprit, which compounds the mystery even further since this person disappears from his normal site leaving behind his belongings. Thus the combination miracle/mystery is never resolved in the popular imagination.

The seven new selections included in *The Day Summer Ended and Other Stories* demonstrate a variety of themes, techniques, and levels of sophistication. As an extension of *Hailstorm and Other Stories*, this is a clear demonstration of Truque's mastery of the art of short-story writing, thematically and structurally. Two of these stories, "The Encounter" and "Two Men," exemplify why there is so much economic despair in Truque's literary world. First of all, there is a system of multinational corporations whose exploitative impact reaches to the lowest echelons of society. Secondly, even small companies are able to exercise an economic stranglehold over the poor by keeping their wages at a defined level of poverty. Strikes are not a viable option because for every opening, regardless of the situation, there are scores of people willing to fill it. Consequently, economics remains the root cause of much of the suffering in Truque's works.

Truque is a writer of many contrasts. The rural optimism expressed in "The Day Summer Ended" is juxtaposed to the urban degradation experienced by the two protagonists of "Two Men." The *campesino* is either the victim of a cruel rural environment or of a city that robs him of his dignity. Yet, in spite of their circumstances, the protagonists do attempt to affirm their being, as can be seen in the preoccupation with *machismo*. This overt manifestation of manliness usually occurs in a situation that ultimately negates its significance, as in "Reveille" and "Two Men."

At the beginning of this chapter, I cited some of Truque's observations concerning his conception of a good short story with the intention of demonstrating how his stories function in relation to his world view. Truque, like Arnoldo Palacios, is from the Chocó, but he extends his literary horizons beyond this limited geographic region. In direct contrast to Palacios, who feels so intensely the plight of the Chocó's people, Truque is an interpreter of all of Colombia. Thus, *Hailstorm* and *The Day Summer Ended* analyze issues crucial to the majority of the population. Truque captures moments crucial in the life of the poor. Survival is perhaps his primary literary motif, with images of death, jails, prostitution, and hunger as internal structural devices.

From the works contained in these volumes, certain conclusions can be drawn concerning characters and settings. In the stories, there is a direct relationship between hunger, irrational acts, and incarceration. Prostitution is another negative symbol equated with dehumanization. The urban environment exacerbates powerlessness and alienation, while the countryside is representative of sterility and violence. In the final analysis, Truque does adhere to his stated goals regarding "qualities of observation, psychological sharpness, and a capacity for synthesis" in capturing many vital moments of existence throughout Colombia.

Finally, in developing his short stories, Carlos Arturo Truque presents a set of literary circumstances without singling out anyone specifically to blame or prescribing a plan of action to be followed. This is in direct contrast to the mode of presentation followed by Arnoldo Palacios. But, most importantly, from an ideological perspective, Truque's characters reflect, to cite Eagleton, "the way men live out their roles in class society, the values, ideas and images which tie them to their social functions and so prevent them from a true knowledge of society as a whole." The poor, uneducated protagonists of *Hailstorm and Other Stories* and *The Day Summer Ended and Other Stories* know that they are suffering but have only vague notions of *why*.

4. The Poet as Novelist

Jorge Artel and Juan Zapata Olivella

Jorge Artel

Born in Cartagena on 27 April 1909 as Agapito de Arcos, Jorge Artel has written one novel, *It's Not Death, It's Dying* (1979), and several volumes of poetry. Artel is best known for *Tambores en la noche* (*Drums in the Night*, 1940), one of the first published contemporary poetic interpretations of Afro-Hispanic culture; *Poemas con botas y banderas* (*Poems with Boots and Flags*, 1972), a critical Marxist assessment, in verse, of Colombian society; and *Antología poética* (*Poetry Anthology*, 1979) a compilation of his best poems.

It's Not Death, It's Dying

It's Not Death, It's Dying is a bitter, pessimistic novel assessing aspects of recent guerrilla movements in Colombia. Out of necessity, the author examines violence, brutality, the gap between rich and poor, human-rights violations, and the possibilities for a revolution. Not surprisingly, the narrative posture concerning the intransigence of Colombian institutions—the Church, the military, the oligarchy—does not change significantly during the course of the narrative development.

Because of the world view implicit in *It's Not Death, It's Dying*, and because of the superior consciousness of the narrator, it is the type of work Stanislaw Eile would label an "auctorial narration." That is to say, the novel embodies, "a lack of intellectual and moral distance between the implied author and the narrator. The latter becomes, therefore, reliable since his information is of an absolute value, and his generalizations determine the cognitive significance of the work as a whole."[1] This is a self-conscious novel in that it interprets a period of history that is very important to Artel and to the development of the Colombian nation. The action of the novel takes place between 1948 and 1966, a period characterized by political violence and guerrilla warfare. *It's Not Death, It's Dying* achieves added significance when viewed as an interpretation of a clearly defined set of extraliterary circumstances. In this regard, Terry Eagleton's comments concerning literature and ideology that were applied to the novels of Arnoldo Palacios are also relevant to Artel to the extent that Eagleton refers to literary works as "forms of perceptions, particular ways of seeing the world; and as such they have a relation to that dominant way of seeing the world which is the 'social mentality' or ideology of an age."[2] *It's Not Death, It's Dying* is certainly not a confirmation of the dominant Colombian ideology during the period that it interprets. Rather, this novel's perception of the world is diametrically opposed to the official social mentality. This is due to the manner in which the auctorial narrator and, by extension, the literary creator express to themselves their relationship to the conditions of their existence.

The novel's plot development begins with the baptism of José Manuel by the local priest. At the time, José is a year old, and those present at the ceremony include José Manuel Neira, his father; Magdalena, his mother; and Lucío Aguirre and his wife, the godparents. On the return to their village, they are confronted by members of an opposing political group. Aguirre dares to speak out on behalf of Neira, who is being beaten. The results are predictable:

—¿Tú también, huevón?—otra vez la voz—¡Ahora mismo, vamos, ya, grite "¡viva el partido conservador, viva el doctor Laureano Gómez, viva el clero!"
—¡Viva el partido liberal, viva el doctor Jorge Eliecer Gaitán!— fue la respuesta del padrino—.[3]

"You also, fucker?" again the voice, "Right now, let's go, shout 'long live the conservative party, long live Doctor Laureano Gómez, long live the clergy'!"
"Long live the liberal party, long live Doctor Jorge Eliecer Gaitán!" was the reply of the godfather.

Aguirre, "the godfather," and the other members of the family are shot for this defiant act. Only Aguirre and the baby, José Manuel, manage to survive this massacre. Aguirre and José Manuel later become important guerrilla leaders; the former dies in battle, and the latter is still fighting at the novel's end.

Only a few of the other characters are clearly drawn. Among them is an important one who weaves in and out of the novel and is identified as "el doctorcito," perhaps the alter ego of the author. The little doctor appears as a kind of social conscience and sounding board for most of the novel's main protagonists, although his true identity is never clarified.

El doctorcito amigo de Lucío Aguirre, profesa como enlace entre los guerrilleros y las más importantes ciudades de la República. Una noche, entró a esta novela diciendo: Hay algo de leyenda en mí, y eso es natural. (p. 24)

The little doctor friend of Lucío Aguirre professes to be a link between the guerrillas and the most important cities of the republic. One night he entered this novel stating: There is the stuff of legend in me, and that is natural.

This character is essential to the self-referential dimension of *It's Not Death, It's Dying* in the sense that this novel refers to itself and to those elements by which it is constituted and communicated. In its auctorial narrative dimension, this work constantly stresses the dynamic interplay between author, work, and reader.

It's Not Death, It's Dying alternates between past and present in its initial pages to construct a plausible set of literary circumstances. The novel's originality is its ability to offer an insider's point of view into the world of the guerrilla. The violence at work in *It's Not Death, It's Dying* is in the form of an organized force against oppression that is sustained by a common goal. The novel's overriding metaphor is death, which is viewed as the supreme sacrifice: "Hay que morir para que otros reciban un país con nuevos sistemas de gobierno y nueva estructura" (It is necessary to die so that others may receive a country with new systems of government and a new structure; p. 106). Just as José Manuel arose from the blood and death of his family, others would certainly follow in his footsteps to bring about social change.

Random acts of violence, in the name of political affiliations, underscore the brutal dimension of *It's Not Death, It's Dying*. Such acts are associated with the modern epoch of "La Violencia," the fratricidal wars in Colombia that began with the assassination of the liberal political leader Jorge Eliecer Gaitán on 9 April 1948, precipitating the *bogotazo*, which has accounted for several hundred thousand deaths and extends to the present day. In this novel, political loyalties are blurred since there is no strict adherence to a particular dogma. Throughout his writings, though, Jorge Artel has made clear his affinity for the political philosophy of Gaitán.

The epoch of "La Violencia" is crucial to the internal coherence of *It's Not Death, It's Dying*. This novel forms a part of the same cultural intertext that has spawned similar interpretations by Arnoldo Palacios and Manuel Zapata Olivella. The images of violence, death, and dying that structure this work unite it to a literary tradition interpreting a set of social circumstances, including guerrilla warfare, that only very recently the Colombian president, Belisario Betancur, sought to change through negotiations.[4]

It's Not Death, It's Dying is a novel of contrasts: between rich and poor, liberals and conservatives, soldiers and guerrillas, traditional and liberated clergy. The Church, the military, and the oligarchy are the three dominant forces that must be changed if the poor are to prosper in Colombia. The first prong of this tripartite repressive force, the Church, is given a balanced presentation in the novel. Some of its representatives are, of course, aligned with the oligarchy and the military, but this is not the case with Camilo Torres, a real-life religious martyr, who appears as a character in *It's Not Death, It's Dying*. Torres, product of a well-to-do family, expressed his doctrine that "Earth's property will belong to the one who works it directly."

In a verbal exchange with a lieutenant who has come to remove suspected guerrillas from his church, Camilo Torres presents his perspective of the movement for change:

Las guerillas tienen una honda raíz social y económica. El pueblo está ávido de reformas agrarias, de reformas sociales, y políticas y mientras el gobierno no satisfaga las necesidades populares y no se comience por decretar una amnistía general, habrá sangre y más sangre . . . . (p. 40)

The guerrillas have deep social and economic roots. The people are eager for agrarian reforms, for social and political reforms, and while the government does not satisfy popular needs and does not begin to declare a general amnesty, there will be more and more bloodshed . . . .

Torres, in this instance and throughout this novel, reiterates the theological doctrines of Pope John and Vatican Council II as well as the encyclicals *Mater et Magistra* (1961) and *Pacem in Terris* (1963). According to Penny Lernoux, in *Cry of the People*, these canons "emphasize the human right to a decent standard of living, education, and political participation . . . John also questioned the absolute right to private property and the Church's unswerving allegiance to capitalist individualism in the cold war against socialist collectivism."[5] The religious doctrine advocated later by the Theology of Liberation, which encouraged physical and spiritual salvation and consciousness-raising among the poor, is very much in evidence throughout *It's Not Death, It's Dying*.

While attempting to put his principles into practice as a member of the Army of National Liberation, Torres dies in his first encounter with the army on 15 February 1966 and becomes a martyr for the revolutionary cause. For the Colombian guerrillas in Artel's novel, Torres is elevated to the level of myth:

Semanas y meses enteros después de su muerte, el padre Camilo Torres estuvo viviendo combatiendo y lanzando proclamas, erigido como un símbolo indestructible en la imaginación del pueblo. Consuelo vago, aunque de profundo significado social. (p. 100)

For entire weeks and months after his death, Father Camilo Torres was alive fighting and issuing proclamations, erect like an indestructible symbol in the popular imagination. A vague consolation, although one of profound social significance.

Since myths are collective and communal, the figure of Camilo Torres provides motivation and sustenance to revolutionary ideals and aspirations, although he is discredited by the rulers in power.

The military is presented as a brutal repressive force in *It's Not Death, It's Dying*. As in many countries in Latin America, the primary mission of Colombia's army is not to defend against outside aggression but to maintain internal law and order. The armed forces unwaveringly follow the chain of command, a view brought out in the exchange between Torres and the Lieutenant: "Usted sabe que los militares cumplimos órdenes . . . Somos unos autómatas . . . El ejército no tiene partido político . . . Ni es deliberante" (You know that military people obey orders . . . we are automatons . . . The army does not have a political party . . . Nor is it a mediator; p. 39). This blind devotion to duty often results in repression, brutality, terrorism, and torture, as demonstrated in the case of the captive Lucío Aguirre, "a human rag," and his companion: "los vendajes sanguinolentos de sus orejas y sus manos sin dedos aun sin cicatrizar, no significaban nada . . . casi nada" (the bloody bandages around his ears and hands without fingers that still had not healed did not mean anything . . . almost nothing; p. 87). This proud military tradition has persisted for centuries.

The oligarchy is a capitalistic social structure that works to benefit its own self-serving financial interests. Negative attitudes toward the oligarchy are elaborated throughout the novel by the anonymous "little doctor," who maintains that a complete change in the existing social and economic systems is in order. Regarding capitalism and underdevelopment, the Doctor refutes many arguments supporting foreign trade and aid. He maintains:

—Al país lo van hundiendo, cada vez más sus deudas con los gringos. Estos fijan el precio de los productos básicos que nos compran, el cual baja a la carrera, mientras el costo de los productos elaborados que ellos nos venden sube indefinidamente. De este modo perdemos más del doble de lo que nos emprestan. La tal Alianza para el Progreso es como masturbarse económicamente. (pp. 59–60)

The country is sinking more and more because of its debts to the gringos. They set the price of raw materials that they buy from us, which go for the minimum, while the cost of finished goods that they sell us rises sky-high. That way we lose more than double of what they loan us. The so-called Alliance for Progress is like economic masturbation.

Ironically, the underdevelopment trap works to the disadvantage of the people who are supposed to be developing. This is not by accident, since the Colombian model applies to most Latin American countries, which were better off economically during the Depression and World War II when they had to bear their own financial burdens than they were when massive amounts of foreign aid were available. Dollars from the International Monetary Fund and the Agency for International Development encourage dependency instead of production. "We are economic colonies of the United States and we have to fight for our own independence," is an apt summation that links Artel to the same view of dependency expressed by Arnoldo Palacios and Carlos Arturo Truque.

A preoccupation with violence and the oligarchy has been constant in the literary production of Artel. Specifically, in *Poems with Boots and Flags*, the poem "April 9th in Colombia" is a lament "To the memory of Jorge Eliecer Gaitán, leader of the Colombian people, assassinated in Bogotá by revolutionary forces, the 9th of April 1948."[6] Eliecer Gaitán, the martyr, is viewed in a positive light:

> Tu pueblo tenía hambre,
> tu pueblo tenía sed,
> tu pueblo vestía harapos
> y en tu perfil de águila
> había inaugurado su esperanza.[7]

> Your people were hungry,
> Your people were thirsty,
> Your people wore rags
> and in your profile of an eagle
> you had initiated their hope.

Artel's vision of all hope for the poor fading with the death of this political figure is reiterated throughout the writer's works. The intimate relationship between leader and people is accentuated by images of solidarity (your people) juxtaposed with those of oppression (hunger, thirst, rags), which makes even more striking the ironic posture of hope.

In the same critical vein, the oligarchy is poeticized in "Poem Not to Be Forgotten."

> Oligarquía: vaca sagrada,
> sistema intestinal y lastre
> de las averiadas estructuras,
> vísceras insaciables y enfermas,
> a gritos pidiendo un cirujano.[8]

> Oligarchy: sacred cow,
> intestinal and food system
> of the damaged structures,
> visceral insatiable and sick,
> begging for a surgeon.

Visceral imagery is effective in presenting this oppressive class of people as a social disease that must be surgically excised by revolution. Like a cancer, they feed on the less powerful members of society who work to support their lifestyle.

Artel's poetic political posture does not change significantly in his three major collections of poetry. His criticism of the oligarchy is apparent in *It's Not Death, It's Dying* as well as in the *Poetry Anthology*, which was also published in 1979. In "This Hard Saltpeter That Reaches My Chest," the poet presents a critical realist view of Colombian society:

> Yo estoy aquí, hundido
> en cualquier ciudad de Colombia,
> viendo golpear y asesinar los estudiantes,
> masacrar indígenas inermes,
> tenderles celadas a las guerrillas.[9]

> And I'm here confounded
> in whatever city of Colombia,
> seeing the beating and assassination of students,

the massacre of unarmed indigenous people
watching over laid-out guerrillas.

Artel is consistent in his call for justice, equality, and change in Colombia's social structure. The violent imagery that appears in his literary creations is replicated, unfortunately, in real life.

In the tradition of the new novel, *It's Not Death, It's Dying* is presented from multiple narrative perspectives. Its truncated discourse reflects the inability of characters to express themselves except in a brutal, violent manner. Violence in this novel is manifested in language, style, and structure. Its cryptic discourse reflects the tension of the narrative as well as the author's search for a creative idiom in which to express this harsh social reality occasioned by the overriding metaphor of death.

It's Not Death, It's Dying is a fragmented novel that draws its internal coherence from themes common to contemporary Colombian literature. Death is a central issue, but, as the title suggests, what is important is not the act of dying but the justifications for making this ultimate sacrifice. For the Colombian poor, there is a perpetual struggle for dignity and a decent way of life. Artel views Colombia as a turbulent country, one whose growth has been stunted by human divisiveness—classist, ethnic, political, and ideological. Unfortunately, he does not offer much hope, since the novel makes it clear that a mere change of government will not cure long-festering social problems. Nor is violence the answer, although it is a means to help bring about social change.

It's Not Death, It's Dying is best discussed in relation to its ideology. Consistent with the definition set forth by Terry Eagleton, this discussion has taken into account "those modes of feeling, valuing, perceiving and believing which have some kind of relation to the maintenance and reproduction of social power." In its perception of the dominant social values and the expressed need for change, *It's Not Death, It's Dying* is similar to *The Jungle and the Rain* by Arnoldo Palacios in the degree that both novels offer alternatives to the status quo.

Neither the rural nor the urban environment holds the key

to a decent existence for the poor. They are victims of institutionalized violence and other attendant symptoms of underdevelopment, including hunger, disease, and the lack of any future. Artel, just as the other Afro-Colombian writers, places the blame where it belongs, with the owners of the country, both inside and outside the nation. The greatest triumph of *It's Not Death, It's Dying* is to provide insight into the culture of the exploited in Colombia while at the same time presenting an alternative response to dependency in that country. In its ability to convey, in novel form, many of the symptoms that lie at the core of guerrilla movements in many countries in Latin America—including Colombia, Peru, and Ecuador—*It's Not Death, It's Dying* is both an exercise in literary Americanism and a search for solutions.

Juan Zapata Olivella

Eighteen years younger than Jorge Artel, Juan Zapata Olivella was born 9 September 1927 in Lorica, in the province of Bolívar. Although only his two novels will be discussed here, he is the author as well of dramas and poetry. His approach to the novel is very different from that of Jorge Artel, as is the level of intensity with which his works are imbued. To the reader of Artel's novels, the degree of bitterness, perhaps based on personal experience, is obvious. On the other hand, Zapata Olivella seeks to inform the reader by presenting a set of literary circumstances and maintaining a narrative distance. Artel and Zapata Olivella are similar, though, in probing the problematic nature of Colombian society, especially the dynamics of social institutions and their impact on individuals. While Artel interprets the national scene, however, Zapata Olivella is concerned primarily with the black experience.

Story of a Black Youth

Story of a Black Youth, Juan Zapata Olivella's first major novel, is steeped in the romantic tradition. It is the story of impossible love between José Prudencio, a black naval cadet who dies at sea while saving the life of a comrade, and Alicia, a white Miss Colombia. Throughout the development of the plot, there are direct references to other romantic masterpieces. Two passages, in particular, are worth quoting. In the first passage, Alicia has become emotionally involved with José and seeks refuge in tradition:

Con frecuencia acostumbraba ir los fines de semana a su pequeña propiedad campestre en los alrededores de la Hacienda El Paraíso, donde y ¡qué casualidad!, se había cumplido un celebre romance, que descrito por Jorge Isaacs con prosa inconfundible, recorrió los caminos del mundo como el más formidable testimonio de una espiritualidad febril.[10]

Frequently she was accustomed to going on weekends to her small country estate in the environs of the El Paraíso Hacienda, where, and what a coincidence!, a famous romance had taken place, which, as described by Jorge Isaacs with unmistakable prose, covered the roads of the world as the most formidable testimony of a feverish spirituality.

The reference here is to Jorge Isaac's *Maria* (1867), Colombia's best romantic novel. In the second passage, while preparing for their first experiences at sea, Mauricio, a colleague of José, is described as including among his reading materials books of all kinds, but the emphasis is placed on a certain category:

A fin de compartirlas con su amigo negro, incluyó a *La María* de Jorge Isaacs por considerarla encarnación clarísima del más sublime idilio de América. También *Amalia* de José Mármol, *Pablo y Virginia*, y aun el tomo que relata las desventuras del joven Werther de Goethe que le sirvieran de consolación espiritual. (p. 190)

With the objective of sharing them with his black friend, he included *María* by Jorge Isaacs, considering it a very clear incarnation of the most sublime idyll of America. Also, *Amalia* by José Mármol, *Pablo and Virginia*, and even the volume that tells the misadventures of young Werther by Goethe, which served them as spiritual consolation.

These references constitute literary intertextuality to the extent that it is defined as a modality of perception, an act of defining texts in the light of other texts. *Story of a Black Youth* is a product of the larger European and romantic cultural intertext that undergirds it.

In spite of its romantic conceptualization, the novel's principal theme is discrimination. José Prudencio is a black cadet who wishes to enter the white world of the Colombian Naval Academy, an institution reserved for the privileged. José cannot be admitted on his own merit and needs the help of Celio Ramírez, a lawyer, and of an independent medical examination to disprove his so-called physical deficiencies. Ramírez's successful defense of José is bolstered by both the commonplace rhetoric of the Civil Rights Movement from the United States and Colombian public outcry. Throughout the process, José Prudencio is presented as larger than life, without a single negative attribute, a presence we would not find in a novel of flesh-and-blood characters. After all, this is a Colombian *Love Story*, not social realist fiction.

A second line of plot development involves the Colombian national beauty contest, in which Alicia Villalonga reigns:

Era tan impresionante su belleza, que muchos turistas, predijeron de inmediato su triunfo, o por lo menos quedar entre las finalistas de mayor opción. Un ducho reportero, aseguró en el micrófono, que nunca, antes había visto una mujer tan linda, y que más que una revelación parecía un milagro de Dios. (p. 124)

Her beauty was so impressive that many tourists predicted her immediate triumph or, at least, her remaining among the most competitive finalists. A clever reporter asserted in the microphone that never before had he seen such a beautiful woman, and that more than a revelation she seemed to be a miracle of God.

Two people of this nature cannot possibly find lasting happiness. They are ideal, romantic abstractions rather than true-to-life personages. Therefore, it is necessary to view them within the romantic canon.

In his discussion of "The Romantic System" under the subheading of "Disillusion," Carlos Bousoño states: "The Romantics were specialists of depression, disenchantment, melancholy." He goes on to observe:

El desengaño frente a la realidad tolera multitud de respuestas, todas diferentes entre sí, en cantidad o cualidad, congruo reflejo de la diversidad humana: melancolía, mayor o menor, matizada, además, personalmente o dolor, o pesimismo, en variación idéntica; o, en fin, acaso, desesperación, que, en la extensa gama de lo posible, puede llegar hasta el suicidio, característica también, nadie lo ignora, de la época. Y es esta tristeza de los románticos, o son esos otros sentimientos aun más graves de su misma familia, los que dan lugar a ciertos temas que pueden expresarlos: el tema de la noche, el de la luna, el de las ruinas, el del amor desgraciado, el de la incomprensión, el de la soledad.[11]

Disillusion faced with reality allows a multitude of answers, all different from each other, in quantity or in quality, a congruous reflection of human diversity: melancholy, greater or lesser, blended personally; or pain, or pessimism, in an identical variation; or, finally, perhaps, despair, which in the vast gamut of possibility, can result in suicide, which nobody would question, is also a characteristic of the era. And it is this sadness of the Romantics, or those other sentiments even more serious of their same family, that give place to certain themes that can express them: the theme of night, of the moon, of ruins, of unfortunate love, of misunderstanding, of solitude.

Since *Story of a Black Youth* is grounded in the romantic tradition, disillusion and its attendant characteristics are essential factors in its world view. Disappointment, melancholy, pain, and pessimism characterize the life of José Prudencio from the moment he appears in the novel until his heroic death at sea. The sea, in this instance, is the final depository of his anguish.

Story of a Black Youth is replete with other romantic themes such as unfortunate love, incomprehension, and solitude. Individual reactions are exacerbated by societal pressures that, in this case, involve the underlying presence of Colombian racism, which makes the relationship between José and Alicia impossible. Therefore, in this novel the determining romantic disease is not tuberculosis, but racism and its ramifications.

José Prudencio's death is handled in true romantic fashion. A consistent image in romantic literature is the *sepulcro*, or tomb. José Prudencio makes reference to this in a letter to Alicia that she reads after his death:

> Fuiste una heroina al entregarme tu amor sin una pizca de prejuicios que tanto daño le hacen a los sueños juveniles. Me llevaré esa entrañable lección de tu espíritu. No renuncies jamás a las sinceriedades de tu corazón, y si te sobrara tiempo, llévame, por favor, unas rosas blancas a mi sepulcro. (p. 204)

> You were a heroine to give me your love without an ounce of the prejudice that does so much damage to juvenile dreams. I will carry that intimate lesson of your spirit. Don't renounce ever the sincerities of your heart, and if you have time left over, bring me, please, some white roses to my tomb.

Alicia's reply to José on his tombstone is "El mar es su tumba, / aquí queda tu recuerdo" (The sea is your tomb, / here remains your memory; p. 205).

Individualism is one of the salient characteristics of the romantic. The predominance of "I" and the propensity for the hero and heroine to occupy center stage are essential to the literary development of the romantic novel. José Prudencio wages a successful battle against most of the obstacles that he encounters, except for one. He is handsome, telling his mother, "puedes estar orgullosa de tener un hijo más hermoso que Mohamed Ali" (you can be proud of having a son more handsome than Mohamed Ali; p. 27); he excels in the academy, "José Prudencio con su inteligencia, su deseo de aprender, su gran imaginación, y su afable carácter, se iba ganando simpatías y afectos" (José Prudencio with his intelligence, his desire to learn, his great imagination, and his friendly nature, was able to win kindness and affection; p. 75); but he is not able to overcome the ultimate obstacle: "Hacía tiempo, mucho tiempo atrás, que José Prudencio había tomado conciencia de las desventajas humanas del color negro de la piel" (It had been a long time, much time had passed, since José Prudencio had taken stock of the human disadvantages of the black color of the skin; p. 112). Therefore, José Prudencio carries individualism to its extreme in an effort to demonstrate that he is worthy of the love and friendship of the majority culture. His death is both a romantic and a human tragedy.

Another critical element of *Story of a Black Youth* is worthy of consideration. Is the novel merely an imitation of romantic themes and motifs, or do its form and content suggest a deeper meaning? One way to approach this question is from the perspective of parody. According to Linda Hutcheon, "parody is a form of imitation, but imitation characterized by ironic inversion, not always at the expense of the parodied text." She notes:

Parody, then, in its ironic "trans-contextualization" and inversion, is repetition with difference. A critical distance is implied between the backgrounded text being parodied and the new incorporating work, a distance usually signaled by irony. But this irony can be playful as well as belittling; it can be critically constructive as well as destructive.[12]

While *Story of a Black Youth* is to a degree an imitation of certain romantic conventions, an exercise in transtextuality, it also interprets concrete social situations. For instance, the allusions by Zapata Olivella to the novel by Isaacs conjure up images of an idyllic Colombian world populated by people who live in peace and harmony unmindful of divisions occasioned by color and class. This harmonic environment is totally inverted by Zapata Olivella, who ironically uses one of the country's most sacred texts, *María*, as a point of departure for embarking on a critically constructive examination of racism and prejudice in Colombia.

Many negative attitudes associated with being black in Colombia surface during the novel's development. Here are but a few examples. The Captain's initial assessment of José Prudencio is "habrá de ser rechazado por cuanto un solo negro que se nos filtre acabaría concediendo privilegios a una raza inaceptable" (he must be rejected because a single black who would infiltrate us would end up conceding privileges to an unacceptable race; p. 14). Doctor Cortina offers his advice while examining José: "ya estamos hasta la coronilla de médicos, abogados, dentistas, y yo agregaría hasta de militares. Usted, por ejemplo con ese cuerpo formidable sería un estupendo deportista. Hay que ver lo que le pagan ahora a un jugador de fútbol" (we are already fed up with doctors, lawyers, dentists, and I would add even military types. You, for example, with that impressive body would be a good athlete. You should see what they pay a good soccer player now; p. 28). Anonymous attitudes include: "Estoy plenamenta identificada contigo. Esos negros llevan algo por encima, o algo por debajo, que enloquece a ciertas mujeres" (I agree fully with you. Those blacks carry something above or something below that drives certain women crazy! p. 179). Don Fernando, Alicia's father, sums up the situation best with a series of rhetorical questions:

¿No crees que tus abuelos se levantarían de sus tumbas si alcanzaran a saber que su nieta estaba decidida a casarse con un descendiente de sus antiguos esclavos? Y acto seguido sin esperar respuesta, continuó: Nuestro sistema de valores es otro, y las debilidades del corazón no pueden pisotear una dignidad ancestral. La vida civilizada exije posturas éticas. ¿Es que podemos acaso aceptar sin remordimientos de conciencia que un negro con un apellido tan común como González, se introduzca así por así, en el seno de una familia tan hidalga? Eres una mujer joven, instruída, y además bellísima, y por lo tanto con todos los atributos para enlazar tu vida con un príncipe, si así lo quisieras. (p. 176)

"Don't you believe that your grandparents would rise up out of their graves if they found out that their granddaughter had decided to marry a descendant of their former slaves?" And without waiting for an answer he continued: "Our system of values is different, and the weaknesses of the heart cannot trample upon ancestral dignity. Civilized life demands ethical postures. Is it that we can possibly accept without remorse of conscience that a black with a surname as common as González would be introduced as such, in the bosom of such a proud family? You are a young woman, learned, and besides very beautiful, with at least all the attributes to marry a prince, if you so desire."

Perceptions of Afro-Colombians run the gamut from the suggestion that they should be confined to their place in society, to the misconception that they should concentrate on sports, to the belief in the sexual prowess of blacks, to the idea of miscegenation weakening the biological fabric of the majority ethnic group. In each instance, the attitudes are erroneous.

The role of nature is essential to the internal coherence of *Story of a Black Youth*. Zapata Olivella is adept at creating metaphoric environments that combine human and natural sentiments. In addition, there is a poetization of the natural milieu throughout the novel in juxtaposition to both positive and negative human sentiments. The tense, emotional scene between José and his mother when they discuss his future ends with the observation, "Reinaba una mañana diafana con un cielo azul y un sol tibio" (A diaphanous day reined with a blue sky and a warm sun; p. 16).[13] The irony of this moment is that nature is oblivious to human emotions as demonstrated in the crisis these characters experience.

On the other hand, when José carries on a romantic interlude with Margorie, a forty-year-old, sympathetic, freckled *gringa*, nature is at peace in a static romantic posture:

El día continuaba alegre como una primavera tropical. El mar lleno de luz y color dejaba sus olas ruidosas en la playa donde los bañistas, cautivados por la música, bailaban sucios de arena, bajo la tibieza de un sol mutilado por las nubes. (p. 53)

The day continued happy like a tropical spring. The sea filled with light and color left its noisy waves on the beach where the bathers, captured by the music, danced dirty with sand, under the warm sun mutilated by the clouds.

This relationship culminates in a fitting manner: "Respiraron hondo la tibieza del verano. Fue entonces cuando enajenados en la embriaguez de la ansiedad se confundieron en una sola sombra negriblanca" (They breathed deeply the warmth of summer. It was then, when estranged in the drunkenness of anxiety, that they lost themselves in a single blackwhite shadow; p. 55). On the other hand, José Prudencio's relationship with Alicia is platonic—in typical romantic fashion. Contrary to popular belief, they do not exchange as much as a kiss, although they are hopelessly enamored. One instance of how they relate to each other is evident in the scene in which Alicia visits José's home, where they have a refreshing drink:

> Hacía realmente calor, y ella con la sabrosa bebida en la mano se suponía que la tomaría despacio, pero demostró tanta sed, que la bebió con apresuramiento y enseguida, pidió más.
> Mientras la miraban, sonreía, una y otra vez, respirando el oxígeno indispensable para mantener quieto a su corazón.
> Afuera el sol palidecía por la acumulación de las nubes. (p. 137)

> It was very warm, and she with the tasty drink in her hand was supposed to drink it slowly, but she was so thirsty, that she drank it rapidly and, then, asked for more.
> While they looked at her, she smiled, once in a while breathing the indispensable oxygen to maintain a calm heart.
> Outside the sun paled with the accumulation of clouds.

This juxtaposing of human sentiments and the natural environment occurs throughout *Story of a Black Youth*. These descriptions are very poetic, reflective of the Zapata Olivella's earlier literary sensibilities and of his affinity for verse. This scene captures an idealized couple who are acted upon by circumstances.

The sea, one of the principal romantic motifs, has a central role in this novel. It is not only the final resting place of José Prudencio, the romantic hero, but also the locale where many emotions are defined and distilled. It is the entity that provides the external structure for the action of the plot from José Prudencio's struggle to get into the academy until his final acts of self definition/destruction.

Story of a Black Youth is composed of numerous oppositions. As Carlos Bousoño points out, "the Romantic loves antithesis, the intensifier always of elements that meet and oppose: antithesis of feelings, of realities, of styles, of attitudes."[14] These contrasts reinforce the inverted romantic values presented by Juan Zapata Olivella. Both the social and the literary contrasts are essential to the world view of this novel, which though a mixture of prose and poetry draws a line separating black from white. Styles and attitudes highlight ethnic differences inherent in Colombian society that do not appear to be reconcilable.

Treading the Ebony Path

Treading The Ebony Path, Juan Zapata Olivella's second novel, recounts the journey of Fulgencio Fernández, a black youth, from his native Colombia to the United States. The classic literary motif of the journey provides the narrator an opportunity to air his opinions concerning Colombian racism and discrimination, violence and revolution in Central America, Zionism and anti-Zionism in the Middle East, as well as a plethora of other human concerns throughout the Americas.

Fulgencio Fernández is another positive Afro-Colombian hero who is driven to self-improvement. Like José Prudencio, he, too, is estranged from a society that sets standards for blacks to equal and then, when they have done so, changes the rules. An "illegitimate son" who is not content with the "bastard condition" of himself and others, Fulgencio strives for the best within societal limitations. He is, unfortunately, faced with some of the same problems as José Prudencio, the protagonist of *Story of a Black Youth*. For Fulgencio:

El color negro sería una rémora difícil de vencer. Con toda clase de pretextos irresponsables se eludía el ordenamiento de las leyes del país. Fue por tercer año consecutivo, que le negaron un cupo en la Facultad de Medicina de la Universidad.[15]

The color black would be a different obstacle to conquer. With all kinds of irresponsible pretexts the mandate of the laws of the country was evaded. For the third consecutive year, they denied him a slot in the University medical school.

Once again, Zapata Olivella uses the pretext of racism and discrimination to launch his protagonist on a journey of self-discovery. Whereas in the case of José Prudencio the process is internal, with Fulgencio it is one of self-exile from the country.

The violence that is an integral part of his upbringing is a constant that Fulgencio cannot escape. His "progenitor," known for his "mirada poética y su vitalidad testicular" (poetic look and testicular vitality), dies a violent death. Despite his unspectacular beginnings, Fulgencio is able to use the motivational factors of his origins to his advantage, so that by the time he is twenty-two "tenía una sólida estructura espiritual, hablaba 3 idiomas, y la maduración de su mente le confirmaba la certidumbre de que todas las razas merecen respeto" (he had acquired a solid spiritual structure, spoke three languages, and the maturation of his mind confirmed to him the certainty that all races warrant respect; p. 20).

Equipped with this pride and self-assurance, Fulgencio embarks on an overland trip to the United States. Due to bureaucratic inefficiency in Bogotá, Fulgencio plans to obtain a visa in Central America, but he learns that he is an undesirable. In Panama the United States vice-consul informs Fulgencio, "estamos saturados de negros" (we're saturated with blacks; p. 25), adding, "para negros nos basta y sobra con los propios" (as far as blacks go, we have enough and are running over with our own; p. 25). On the other hand, Cuqui, Fulgencio's white Costa Rican lover, is given a visa when she promises to grant sexual favors to the official.

The journey of Fulgencio is modeled on aspects of the black diaspora throughout the Americas. This dimension is revealed at a conference he attends at which a preacher from the United States stresses positive aspects of the Afro-American experience. Much of the credit for keeping alive aspects of Afro-American culture is given to creative writers, and rightly so. The preacher remarks:

En cambio, debo reconocer que los poetas desde los cubanos hasta los de Surinam son nobles liberadores del oscuro contexto humano de los descendientes del Africa. Con sutileza lírica exaltan sus virtudes en el brevario de un verso. (p. 76)

On the other hand, I must recognize that poets from the Cubans to those of Surinam are noble liberators of the dark human context of the descendants from Africa. With lyric subtlety they exalt their virtues in the context of verse.

He then delves into the Afro-American cultural intertext to

cite poems from Nicolás Guillén and Langston Hughes depicting suffering and resistance that ultimately result in cultural survival. "Y encontró al negro descalzo. / Desnudo el cuerpo llagado sobre el campo" (And he found the black man barefooted. / Naked of body wounded in the field; p. 76) in Cuba evolves into "Me mandan a comer a la cocina cuando llegan las visitas; / Pero yo me río, y como bien y crezco fuerte" (They order me to eat in the kitchen when company comes; / but I laugh, and eat well and grow strong; p. 77) in the context of the United States. This, in essence, has been the history of black survival throughout the Americas, with degradation turning to cultural maroonage. The reader's perception of the connection between the literature of Guillén, Hughes, and Zapata Olivella strengthens common bonds among both readers and writers.

The trip through each country provides an opportunity for the narrator to share insights into recent history in Central America. For instance, in El Salvador one issue involves the murder of United States religious people. In Guatemala it is the violence of the guerrilla war juxtaposed to the culture of that country. Guatemala is the culminating point of Fulgencio's journey. He is detained, tortured, humiliated, and finally freed after international protest, thereby living out a literary fantasy: "El jet de la fuerza érea norteamericana lo llevaría a Chicago donde lo esperaban sus hermanos negros" (The jet of the North American Air Force would carry him to Chicago where his black brothers were waiting for him; p. 190).

In Guatemala, *Treading the Ebony Path* reaches its climax. It is here, too, that the novel's narrative thread comes undone and unravels in many directions. Interspersed with an episode devoted to the kidnaping of Orson Welles are a recounting of a Jewish prisoner's experiences in the Middle East and a commentary on Guatemalan concentration camps. An observation that the narrator makes concerning Guatemala is applicable to much of Central America during this period in terms of brutality, instability, and extremism. Innocent people have no protection from state-sponsored terrorism and violence. Part of the solution to the problem resides in each person's ability to find positive cultural heroes from the past who will provide the inspiration for armed resistance and social change.

In *Story of a Black Youth* and *Treading the Ebony Path*, Juan Zapata Olivella takes a different approach to the Afro-Colombian experience than did either Palacios or Artel. The first works by both Zapata Olivella and Palacios are grounded in a European literary tradition, naturalism and romanticism respectively, and achieve the expected results. The struggle in Zapata Olivella's fiction does not reach the level of profundity found in the novels of Palacios and Truque, but his aims are different. Although Zapata Olivella represents the positive in the Afro-Colombian experience, by showing that positive destroyed by oppressive forces, his message advocating change rings as clear as that of his counterparts.

The literary works of Juan Zapata Olivella are a negation of the dominant social ideology in their exploration of the relationship of Afro-Colombians to the larger society. The author is critical of the type of internal psychological violence and discrimination that has historically damaged blacks and relegated them to inferior social positions. Juan Zapata Olivella stresses the need for self-pride and psychical liberation to help alleviate inherent and unyielding social pressures.

5. From Oppression to Liberation
Manuel Zapata Olivella

Manuel Zapata Olivella is one of Colombia's leading men of letters. He was born in Lorica, Córdoba, on 17 March 1920, and, in addition to being a writer, is a doctor, anthropologist, folklorist, and professor. In addition to a volume of short stories, his publications include seven novels: *The Drenched Earth* (1947), *10th Street* (1960), *Behind the Mask* (1963), *Chambacú, a Black Ghetto* (1963), *In Chimá a Saint Is Born* (1964), *Changó, the Great SOB* (1983), and *El fusilamiento del Diablo* (*The Execution of the Devil*, 1986). The first six novels are my focal point. During the three decades encompassed by these works, there has been a perceptible development in Zapata Olivella's narrative art in terms of form, content, and world view. His early work followed basically two lines of development: the social-realist public-service-type of narrative evident in *The Drenched Earth* and *10th Street*, and the Afro-Colombian and mythic directions that began in *Chambacú, a Black Ghetto* and *In Chimá a Saint Is Born* and evolved more fully in *Changó, the Great SOB*. *Behind the Mask* serves as a work of synthesis for Zapata Olivella's early literary production.

Zapata Olivella's novels assess the different strata of Colombian society, but he dwells mostly on the underdogs—the rural *campesino* in *The Drenched Earth* and *In Chimá a Saint Is Born*, the urban street people in *10th Street*, and the dispossessed city blacks in *Chambacú, a Black Ghetto*. *Behind the Mask* is a psychological integration of both the rural and the urban experiences, while *Changó, the Great SOB* is an epic that embraces black people throughout the Americas. My approach in tracing the novelistic output of Zapata Olivella from *The Drenched Earth* to *Changó, the Great SOB* will entail a discussion of the relationship between form and content as well as an interpretation of violence, ideology, and world view that is in keeping with my approach to Afro-Colombian fiction.[1]

Violence and oppression are both prominent unifying literary themes in the works of Manuel Zapata Olivella. As I have demonstrated in my discussion of the other Afro-Colombian writers, oppression is the result of societal structures that have been in place for centuries in Colombia, supported by the tripartite repressive force of the Church, the oligarchy, and the military. Not all of Zapata Olivella's novels deal with the well-known epoch of La Violencia, Colombia's fratricidal killings begun in 1948, although *10th Street* is situated in this era. The violence in Zapata Olivella's works does comprise both the vertical (or social) and horizontal (or individual) dimensions as they were defined earlier.

If we briefly consider Zapata Olivella's works dealing with two of his major themes, the rural *campesino* and the urban *negro*, we can see that a significant pattern emerges. In *The Drenched Earth*, for instance, the *campesinos* do not have the solution to the problem of oppression. In *In Chimá a Saint Is Born*, its counterpart, armed resistance is the answer. In *10th Street* the urban dwellers do not encounter an alternative to the intolerable conditions under which they exist. Yet in *Chambacú, a Black Ghetto*, armed resistance is the alternative to the problems of violence, hunger, oppression, and dehumanization rampant in Chambacú. A brief examination of each novel will demonstrate how oppression and liberation as two thematic poles temper Zapata Olivella's world view and function in his literary creations. This discussion will also examine in his novels, following Terry Eagleton's critical perspective, "those modes of feeling, valuing, perceiving and believing which have some kind of relation to the maintenance and reproduction of social power" in Colombia.

The Drenched Earth

The Drenched Earth was not well received when it was first published in Colombia. Francisco José González criticized it for both its ideological content and its anticlerical tones.

González observed: "Poor Don Manuel Zapata Olivella, perhaps an innocent victim of the marxism spread in books, magazines, and pamphlets for use by the intellectual middle class." He added, in defense of the Church: "The Church founded this nation. Intellectually all that is Colombia is owed to the Church: the best works, the best universities, the best schools, have not only been Catholic but also ecclesiastical." González concluded by reacting to the book's world view and artistic merit: "His book, the doctrinal part, has resulted in an unjust and vulgar diatribe. As literature, it does not fail to have some merit."[2] This reaction is typical of observations afforded *The Drenched Earth* in Colombia. Critics tended to praise the aesthetic quality of the novel while criticizing its ideological posture. This work is often categorized as a "novel of the earth" because of its content and the way in which the plight of the *campesino* is presented.

In a paper prepared for the Seminario Andrés Bello, Gloria Durán Salcedo devotes most of her attention to *costumbrista* aspects of *The Drenched Earth*. She also discusses the "Ideological Content" in two pages. She equates ideology with theme, beginning her discussion by stating: "Two fundamental ideas are apparent in the work: earth and myth."[3] Although she does not discuss "ideology" as such, Durán Salcedo leaves the impression that, in spite of not wanting to dwell on the novel's basic thrust, she understands Zapata Olivella's interpretation: "The work is a sociological document, one that denounces a current event, which is the trampling by the powerful of the weak."[4] This brief analysis by Durán is a good basic formalist introduction to *The Drenched Earth*.

With *The Drenched Earth*, Zapata Olivella began his long literary career by championing the cause of the underdog from an insider's perspective. Hence his novel is one of the most authentic literary interpretations of the Sinú River Basin available. Fanny Paez de Rivera has taken the analysis of Zapata Olivella's works one step further in her thesis "Los Personajes Reales en la Novelística de Manuel Zapata Olivella" ("Real Personages in the Novels of Manuel Zapata Olivella"). Paez de Rivera found real-life prototypes for the fictional characters Corrillito, El Culebro, Felipe Espitia, and Marco Olivares. But more important than the direct relationship between fictional and real characters is the fact that *The Drenched Earth* is representative of the work of an author who is able to capture the experiences of the Colombian population from the perspective of an Afro-Hispanic writer committed to change.

The Drenched Earth is essentially a novel of humans against nature. It chronicles a battle waged by the *campesinos* of the Sinú River Basin, in the rice patties of rural Colombia, against both the human and the natural orders. *The Drenched Earth* attests to the personal determination and fortitude of Gregorio Correa (el viejo Goyo) and his people against the rich landowner Jesús Espitia, the church, and the armed forces. In this instance, good does not triumph over evil; instead, the issue of land ownership is left unresolved in a realistic manner. Although Correa, who is forced by Espitia to leave his tillable land, wins a few moral and physical battles, no significant structural changes occur from the moment Correa and his uprooted family establish themselves on the tributaries until the final destruction of their huts. Although their struggle is viewed in a heroic mode, it does not better the lot of other *campesinos* in the region.

The Drenched Earth explores both positive and negative aspects of the rural experience. There is the negative emphasis on exploitation, dependency, and repression, while the author views in a positive light the capacity for resistance and survival, manifestations of popular culture, and the process of miscegenation.

In *The Drenched Earth* the characters are composed of a cross section of the population:

El cuerpo de Gregorio relucía su alquitranada piel al lado de la seca y mohosa de Próspero, que era indio, sin saberlo. Su compadre, mulato, también ignoraba su ancestro africano. Ellos eran simples campesinos nacidos y criados a orillas del Sinú.[5]

The body of Gregorio shone its blackened skin alongside the dry and musky skin of Próspero, who was Indian, without knowing it.

His partner, mulatto, also, did not know of his African ancestry. They were plain country folks born and raised on the banks of the Sinú.

Ethnicity is an issue throughout *The Drenched Earth* since ancestry and different shades of color are used to discriminate socially and economically among the population. While heredity is not an issue between Gregorio and his cohorts, it is an important factor in the superiority complex of the oppressors, Jesús Espitia and el Mono, his son:

> Algo más que el dinero y la posición social separaba al Mono Espitia de la tripulacion, ese algo era su raza. Nadie ignoraba su ascendencia sajona y el segundo matrimonio de su madre con Jesús Espitia. También repudiaban a éste su afán de esconder su color negro. Nadie fuera de él mismo, había extrañado su piel; era hijo de negros y desde niño lo vieron renegrido como carbón. Pero él se preguntaba a diario frente al espejo de dónde y cuándo surgieron el tinte oscuro, los labios gruesos y la nariz chata como almeja. Deseoso de tener descendientes rubios, se había casado con la viuda yanqui. Pero todas las precauciones del negro Jesús Espitia fracasaron, porque precisamente el Mono, hijo del primer matrimonio, costó la fecundidad a la madre, que, preocupada por la fortuna del nuevo pretendiente, lo había ocultado. Los años transcurrieron y el marido comenzó a comprender el mal negocio. De ahí que a la postre, y sin esperanza de tener un hijo de ella, optó por darle su apellido al hijastro, existiendo de hecho el primer Espitia blanco. (pp. 135-36)

> Something more than money and social position separated Mono Espitia from his peers, that something was his race. Nobody forgot his Saxon heritage and the second marriage of his mother to Jesús Espitia. They also repudiated the latter because of his affinity for hiding his black color. Nobody outside of himself (Jesús) had felt his skin strange; he was the son of blacks and since childhood they saw him as jet black as coal. But he asked himself daily in front of the mirror from where and when had this dark color, the thick lips, and the flat nose like a clam come? Desirous of having blond descendants, he had married the Yankee widow. But all the precautions of black Jesús Espitia went awry, because precisely Mono, the first son of the marriage, cost the fecundity of the mother, who, preoccupied with the fortune of the new suitor, had hidden him.

The years passed and the husband began to understand the bad deal. From then on and without the hope of having a child by her, he settled for giving his surname to his stepson, creating in fact the first white Espitia.

Jesús Espitia and his family consistently denied the process of *mestizaje*, which is a biological fact of the region, while enriching themselves, monopolizing the land, and acquiring titles of nobility. Jeús manifests a type of self-hate that is evident in societies where no positive value is attributed to blackness. For him the people who have to be exploited are those of color.

Most of the characters in this novel have respect for, and close identification with, the natural environment. Correa views his initial uprooting and exile in relation to the current of the river: "y he aquí que de repente él mismo se veía arrastrado hacia ese destino incierto, a esa ruta por donde se iban los seres y las cosas que no resistían su avalancha" (and here suddenly he saw himself dragged toward that uncertain destiny, to that route along which went beings and things which did not resist its avalanche; p. 25). His future as a rice farmer at the mouth of the tributaries carries no guarantees because of the changing flow of the currents. However, due to hard work and perseverance, Correa's skepticism changes as he is able to alter the dictates of nature:

Contento de qúe todo marchaba bien, quiso volver a la cama, pero fuerzas extrañas lo retuvieron. La tierra, la afinidad de su cuerpo con el agua y el aliento de la noche, lo uncían a los elementos que se combinaban en él como vientre de los ámbitos, manteniéndolo despierto, vivo, alerta. En esa hora tuvo la impresión de que definitivamente se habría enraizado en Los Secos, igual que las matas de arroz, que hundían sus raíces con firmeza y elevaban sus tallos por encima de las aguas. (p. 89)

Content that everything was going well, he wished to return to bed, but outside forces detained him. The earth, the affinity of his body with the water and spirit of the night, tied him to the elements that combined in him like the belly of the environment, keeping him awake, alive, alert. In that hour he had the impression that definitively he had established roots in Los Secos, just like the rice plants, which had buried their roots with firmness and raised their stalks above the waters.

This human/telluric identification represents the epitome of respect and harmony between the human and natural orders. The fusion of body and spirit with Mother Earth, which has provided sustenance, accentuates the permanency of Correa and his cohorts.

The Drenched Earth stresses the importance of popular culture in the lives of these *campesinos*. The cockfight, song and dance, and oral tradition are alive and well in Los Secos. Carrillito, whose "algarabía de mulato provocaba recordaciones en los viejos y avivaba el amor de los jóvenes" (mulatto riddles provoked memories in the old and revived love in the young; p. 74), is a popular hero, a *coplista* whose influence permeates the region. Correa is known for his story-telling ability, which keeps alive the oral tradition, usually in the form of animal stories involving tigers and rabbits, bulls and crocodiles. Correa's house is also the center of other cultural activities involving song, dance, and music.

Muchos de ellos tenían ancestro africanos y no pocos de indio, pero unos y otros se asomaban a las notas de la gaita indígena como si la sangre floreciera en el canto montuno de la flauta. (p. 114)

Many of them had African ancestry and not a few had Indian, but some of them moved to the notes of the indigenous *gaita* as if blood flourished in the untamed song of the flute.

This particular synthesis of the indigenous *gaita* with the African *tambor* produces the music for the *cumbia*, one of the most authentic of Colombian dances and one that reflects national cultural syncretism. Throughout *The Drenched Earth*, in spite of the never-ending obstacles, Zapata Olivella's protagonists are presented with their identity and culture intact.

The appearance of Marco Olivares, schoolteacher, lends an intellectual and a political perspective to the struggle against oppression. He is an astute organizer and practitioner of invective:

—¡Hermanos campesinos! ¡Labriegos explotados! ¡Madres sufridas! A ustedes les pregunto: ¿Quién ha robado sus tierras? ¿Quién los hace trabajar como a bestias y los mantiene bajo la explotación? Jesús Espitia, el amo cruel, que roba y deshonra a sus hijas. El verdugo que incendia y destroza los sembrados de ustedes para arruinarlos y convertirlos en sus esclavos . . . .
—Ustedes conocen mi honradez y mi pobreza—decía—; soy hijo del pueblo, soy de vuestra propia carne y por eso combato a Espitia, que los oprime. Contra él y el señor cura, que patrocina sus hijos espurios, debemos levantar nuestros puños. Acabemos con su tiranía y terminará el crimen, la impudicia y la explotación. (p. 175)

"Fellow *campesinos*! Exploited laborers! Suffering mothers! I ask you: Who has stolen your lands? Jesús Espitia, the cruel owner, who steals and dishonors your daughters. The hangman who burns and destroys your crops in order to ruin you and convert you into slaves . . . .
"You know about my honesty and my poverty," he said; "I am a son of the people, I am of your very own flesh and for that reason I battle Espitia, who oppresses you. Against him and the priest, who patronize their spurious children, we must raise our fists. Let's finish this tyranny and end the crime, the immodesty, and the exploitation."

Although he is wounded in this episode in an assassination attempt, Olivares survives to organize a successful labor union and to serve as a general social conscience until he is ousted by the combined efforts of Church and oligarchy due to his class and economic views. On the other hand, Olascuaga, the priest, wages an active battle for the minds of his flock, whom he does not want to be socially educated. When Olivares is charged with being a Communist, his reaction is that he acts in "defensa de los intereses del pueblo" (defense of the interests of the people; p. 187). Since the authorities will not tolerate anybody who places the people's interests above those of the rulers, the *campesinos* cannot possibly win the war against their oppressors. The belief that has been instilled in the inhabitants of Los Secos is: "Era mejor morir combatiendo que perecer destripado como lombriz sin rebeldía" (It was better to die fighting than to perish gutted like a tame worm; p. 224). José Darío puts these ideas into practice when he kills el Mono Espitia, who has raped José's wife, María Teresa, who gives birth to a "white" child.

The trajectory of Olivares is very similar to that of Caimacán in *The Stars Are Black*. They both realize that violence is the only true option for the oppressed but, due to structural elements inherent in the society, are unable to implement force to bring about meaningful change.

The ultimate downfall of the people of Los Secos, however, is brought about by an indifferent Nature. Drought causes the Sinú to change its course, and subsequent erosion from the intrusion of seawater destroys the rice crop. The people are resourceful enough to move their community to the mouth of the bay of Cispata to renew their fight for survival. Jesús Espitia takes over the unproductive lands they have abandoned and finds no logical explanation for his failure to prosper there. The narrator surmises:

Cosas de brujo. He aquí la verdad de aquella paradoja. El viejo Goyo y las familias de Los Secos subsistieron en la desembocadura con pura brujería. Lo que saben los hombres fuertes cuando están enfrentados al dilema de vida o muerte. Un verdadero milagro les permitió sobrevivir en tan precario medio y otro, no menos sobrenatural, les animó a convertir en tierras habitables la cenagosa desembocadura. Ahora las dejaban para que otros, asalariados y sumisos, intentaran repetir la hazaña. El viejo Goyo sabía que el Sinú no lo permitiría. (p. 262)

Witchcraft. Herein lies the truth of that paradox. Old Goyo and the families of Los Secos subsisted in the river's mouth with pure witchcraft. That which strong men know when they are confronted with the dilemma of life and death. A true miracle permitted them to survive in such a precarious environment and another, no less supernatural, motivated them to convert into habitable land the swamplike opening. Now they left it so that others, salaried and submissive, would intend to repeat the feat. Old Goyo knew that the Sinú would not permit it.

At the beginning of this discussion, I cited a review of *The*

Drenched Earth that refers to the novel as having, "in the doctrinal part, . . . resulted in an unjust and vulgar diatribe." The character of Marco Olivares carries the ideological brunt of the novel and calls for justice instead of revolution. After Olivares is fired, he establishes an alternative school with a clearly defined mission:

> . . . cuando los campesinos regresaban de sus labores, los recibía para hablarles de temas que les despertaban su conciencia de proletarios y el ejemplo de su propia escuela le servía para revelarles su poderío, siempre que unieran y fortalecieran sus intereses. (p. 254)

> . . . when the *campesinos* returned from their chores, he received them in order to talk to them about topics that awakened their conscience as proletarians, and the example of his own school served to reveal to them their power, as long as they were unified and strengthened their interests.

Olivares's mission is precisely to help them determine why they function as they do in a society so hung up on class and ethnicity. Easy answers do not appear to be forthcoming.

As a work of art, *The Drenched Earth* is certainly not "mysteriously inspired." It is an interpretation of social perceptions, based on the fictional presentation of characters and circumstances, and, as such, represents the manner in which the author views the continuing struggle of the *campesinos* of the Sinú River Basin.

In Chimá a Saint Is Born

Significantly, the fifteen years that separate *The Drenched Earth* and *In Chimá a Saint Is Born* reflect a meaningful change in ideology from the attempts in the former novel to modify the economic structure by Socialist rhetoric, strikes by salaried workers, and individual acts of heroism to the collective open armed rebellion in *In Chimá a Saint Is Born*.

In the later novel, the author constructs his fictional world along the northern coastal marshland of Colombia. In Chimá, the setting, a cult of religious fanaticism grows up around an invalid, Domingo Vidal, who is miraculously saved from a burning hut by a priest, Father Berrocal. The citizens of the village, in grave need of mental escape and immediate solutions to their human problems, rally around Domingo, the "savior," for comfort.

This, however, creates a problem for organized religion, which responds through its advocates by trying to suppress the idolatry that becomes rampant in the town. A crisis develops when the Church and the military resort to repressive measures against the villagers, who react in turn. It is during this crisis that these people realize that they, too, have power. Oppression and a need to develop new myths and ways of looking at one's circumstances are but two of the themes of *In Chimá a Saint Is Born*; rebellion is another.

Thematically, the novel examines the attempts of an oppressed people to give meaning to existence. This is exemplified in both the spiritual and the physical relationships of protagonists. Different interpretations of the fire incident help provide various resolutions to individual needs. To enhance his reputation, in subsequent years Domingo performs several miracles and cures through a series of time-tested remedies and through luck. The problems that he resolves are associated with ghosts, fertility, and insanity.

After his death at the symbolic age of thirty-three, due to exposure to the elements, Domingo's stature grows even larger in the popular imagination. The situation in Chimá is succinctly presented by the narrator: "La supersticion y la religiosidad son dos mundos contradictorios que se complementan" (Superstition and religiosity are two contradictory worlds that complement each other).[6] The novel's particular mixture of superstition with religion reveals the incongruous nature of the villagers' worship. There is a constant vacillation between Church and idol in the effort to solve immediate problems.

As the boycott of organized religion begins, when Domingo cannot be buried at the altar, the sacristan Jeremías emerges as the "Prophet" to further fan the fires of imagination. He preaches, along with Belaude, Domingo's sister, throughout the territory, extolling the miracles of Domingo—first to build his own image and later because he is a true believer. All doubts in the popular mentality concerning Domingo's qualifications for sainthood are erased when, two years after burial, his body is uncovered intact, mummified. After a brief display in the church, Domingo's body is quartered by Father Berrocal and his cohorts. This act is interpreted by the *campesinos* as an assassination, which motivates them to fight for their beliefs.

In Chimá the battle is for psychological, spiritual, and physical liberation. These desires are projected through the people's adoption of Domingo as an immediate solution to their problems. They are seeking their just rewards on this earth and not in the hereafter. The Chimaleros' creation and construction of the myth of Domingo Vidal is based on the archetype of Christ and on biblical mythology. He is a symbolic projection of their hopes and values, and he binds the community together in its many moments of crisis. They do need an immediate source of strength for the daily hardships that they face. Domingo temporarily fulfills this need and also provides the impetus for rebellion. As a Christ-like figure who stands for all that is good, Domingo is placed in opposition to the Church, which governs, for the most part, by fear and intimidation.

Father Berrocal is shown to oppose violent methods of bringing his constituents to their senses, even for the sake of Catholicism. His negative reply to the offer of force by the *alcalde*, don Cipriano Botero, is indicative of this attitude. Berrocal maintains this antiviolent paternalistic attitude throughout, as he is constantly faced with converting the villagers back to his type of religious reality. His intolerance of anything except official Christianity is reflected in a system of values that entails persecution of the villagers. After Father Berrocal dies of natural causes, Botero blames the villagers and attacks them. It is during the ensuing battles that he, representing authority, realizes the revolutionary potential of the Chimaleros.

Comprenden que el pueblo tiene necesidad de un pretexto para luchar y con aquellos machetes y escopetas serían capaces de realizar mayores portentos que todos los atributos a Domingo Vidal. (p. 144)

They understand that the people need a pretext to fight and with those machetes and shotguns they would be capable of achieving more goals than all of those attributed to Domingo Vidal.

Thus the novel closes on a positive note, as there is an awareness on the part of both officials and villagers of the latent power of the latter. As presented in *In Chimá a Saint Is Born*, the most effective method of alleviating oppression both spiritual and physical is by the development of new myths and by rebellion against structures imposed from the outside.

In Chimá a Saint Is Born conveys an air of optimism. Its major triumph is to advance the idea that force can be used to break the hold that the military and the Church exercise over the masses of Latin America. Zapata Olivella's message is that when the rural poor realize that they can wield power too, perhaps they will be able to control their own destinies. The difference between this novel and *The Drenched Earth* is that the miracle of Gregorio Correa, unlike those of Domingo Vidal, never transcends the heroic stage to reach the mythic. Therefore, its potential as a force for change is very limited. In Chimá the *campesinos* finally realize that it takes a meshing of the spiritual and the physical in order to mitigate their circumstances. This is precisely the route they follow in order to determine their own destiny.

A similar evolution in world view is evident in the urban environment of *10th Street* and *Chambacú, a Black Ghetto*, two radically different novels that are representative of the violent trends in Colombian letters. In *10th Street*, violence as a theme does not evolve from horizontal in-group brutality and random killing during the Gaitán epoch to vertical-social violence for change. This novel presents the inner dynamics of poverty, hunger, and oppression as they are experienced by the street people of Bogotá.

10th Street

About *10th Street*, Agustín Rodríguez observes:

En todo caso, esta obra no logra superar en ninguna forma otras producciones de Zapata Olivella, se ha trazado una línea monocorde sobre las injusticias sociales y por este sendero echa a andar su humanidad paralítica y la grosería de ese mundo, que debe ser redimido, claro está, pero por un cristianismo activo lejos de toda intención política.[7]

In any event, this work does not manage to supersede in any form other productions of Zapata Olivella; a monochord line has been traced over social injustices and along this path walks his paralytic humanity and the grossness of that world, which must be redeemed, rightly so, but by an active Christianity far from all political intention.

With an attitude similar to that in the review of *The Drenched Earth* cited at the beginning of this chapter, Rodríguez wants Zapata Olivella to put more faith in religion and less in politics. The author has implicitly demonstrated through his world view that the Church is not an effective agent of social change due to its historical alliance with the oligarchy in Colombia.

The criticism of *10th Street* offered by Wanda Caruso is much more direct. Her two major objections are: "In *10th Street* we find a defective although original technique whose main error is confusion" and "the language of this novel leaves much to be desired in its grammatical aspect. There are many poorly used sentences, incongruences, and confusions." Caruso points out the omission of the "personal A" on two occasions by the author to substantiate her observation that "his preparation as a novelist was deficient."[8] She is more concerned with form than with content.

On the other hand, in his discussion of authors' political concerns and how they are emphasized in literature in Colombia, Argentina, and Cuba, John S. Brushwood asserts that *10th Street* is "one of the most vital political novels."[9] This novel is political to the degree that it places fictional characters in a clear historical frame that facilitates our interpretation of reality. The basic ideological thrust of *10th Street* is for change in the social structure; the method employed to bring this about is what the novel questions. Intertextually, *10th Street* and the urban experience in *The Jungle and the Rain* both interpret the violence of the *bogotazo*.

In "La Semilla" ("The Seed"), the first section of the novel, the reader experiences street life among the homeless, the destitute, the dehumanized. Hunger is the basis for social unrest, as people are willing to rob, kill, sell their bodies, and more in order to survive. Characters like "El Pelúo," the nameless *gamines*, "Sargento," "Malicia," "Garrapata," "Viruta," and others that we meet early on lead a miserable existence. "Mamatoco," the boxer, and "Tamayo the poet," editors of *La Voz del Pueblo*, a newspaper, believe erroneously that they have revolutionary potential. However, with the advent of "La Violencia" of 1948, which is presented in the novel's second section, "La Cosecha" ("The Harvest"), the poet realizes that there is a difference between the theory and practice of revolution.

10th Street is structured around metaphors of death and dying. The novel's opening scene focuses on El Pelúo and his agony at the death of his wife, Saturnina. The book's closing episode presents a panoramic view of the carnage of the ill-fated armed mass rebellion. The dehumanization of the majority of the street people through poverty, hunger, and prostitution is a principal motif in *10th Street*. Parmenio awakens his family with the cry "—¡Abran los ojos, mis hijos! ¡Hoy hay más hambre que ayer" ("Open your eyes, my children! Today there is more hunger than yesterday!")[10] El Pelúo's wife is taken to the Medical School and dissected because he cannot afford to bury her: "había perdido el hábito de usar dinero" (he had lost the habit of using money; p. 13) Rengifo, a policeman who left the army because he could not tolerate the fevers, reflects: "Pero el hambre de la ciudad era tan terrible o más que el paludismo" (But the hunger of the city was as terrible as or worst than malaria; p. 54). Thus hunger is raised to the same level of intensity as in *The Stars Are Black*.

The motif of prostitution is the focus between Laboriel, a medical student and son of one of the most respected families in Bogotá, and two prostitutes, La Pecosa and Rosita. Laboriel is a guilt-ridden figure who tries to cleanse his mind by overpaying the women and hoping that he does not contract venereal disease. La Pecosa and Rosa manage to strip off the class facade that separates them from Laboriel, informing him that in sexual manners they are at the same level of dehumanization. Rosita's assertion is, "Aquí se es sinvergüenza desde el momento en que se entra" (Here one is a son of a bitch from the moment he enters; p. 71).

Although the prerequisites for vertical violence are there in the dispossession and declassification of the masses, the motivating incident for collective destruction is the murder of Mamatoco by unidentified assailants. Mamatoco, the black ex-boxer, and Tamayo, the poet, see the paper *Voz del Pueblo* as an instrument that "denunciará la prostitución del capitalismo" (will denounce the prostitution of capitalism; p. 38). It is a fact sheet that prints what official newspapers dare not. Consequently, Mamatoco's death is interpreted as a political crime: "Aquí no se ha matado un hombre, se ha herido de muerte a un pueblo" (Here a man has not been killed, a people has been wounded to death; p. 80).

The ensuing mass violence results in one of the most striking ironies of the "revolution" called for by Tamayo:

En el estrecho espacio de la chichería, el poeta Tamayo se afanaba en organizar la revolución, pero él que tantas veces había hablado de ella, de capitanear las masas, en aquel momento decisivo no tenía nada organizado que ofrecer al gran pueblo dispuesto a seguirlo. Se retorcía las barbas, se metía las manos en los cabellos y se quedaba mirando el cadáver de la ventera, de su querida Tomasa. (pp. 95-96)

In the narrow space of the bar, Tamayo, the poet, worked to organize the revolution, but he who so many times had talked about it, of leading the masses, in that decisive moment had nothing organized to offer the great mass of people ready to follow him. He twisted his beard, ran his fingers through his hair, and remained staring at the corpse of the innkeeper, his dear Tomasa.

Tamayo, it seems, is an intellectual revolutionary instead of a man of action. But, because he is the only one capable of articulating their sentiments, the masses follow him until the fatal end.

There is a grotesque, esperpentic quality to *10th Street* that is accentuated by the misery of the street people, the image of El Pelúo bearing a coffin containing the decomposing remains of his wife and son, the joy of the prostitutes sharing a drink with money they have overcharged a rich customer, and finally the disjointed images of reality projected in the novel. Zapata Olivella interprets the economic situation of the urban masses as being insoluble but nonetheless composed of a great deal of revolutionary potential. It will, however, take more than a misguided intellectual to steer the people on the right course.

What Tamayo views as a revolution is really a fratricidal war between liberals and conservatives in which the masses are used as fodder. The enthusiasm for change first held by the downtrodden quickly degenerates into indiscriminate looting and murder. Rengifo, one of the few positive characters, presents a final revealing assessment:

Comenzó a tener exacta proporción de la masacre. En el momento de la lucha cuando veía caer a su lado a desconocidos y compañeros, miraba las bajas como algo normal que le encendían el heroismo y la indignación. Pero ahora sus ojos se habían empequeñecido o los muertos aumentaban; su mirada no alcanzaba a abarcarlos a todos, ni su mente a imaginarse su cuantía. Le entró dolor horrible porque esas vidas hubieran sido sacrificadas inutilmente. Vislumbraba entonces el alcance de la traición. Si los jefes que se decían representar al pueblo no hubieran pactado con el gobierno tambaleante, tal vez habría habido mucho más muertos, el doble o el triple, pero cada uno de ellos hubiera justificado su sacrificio. (pp. 125-26)

He began to get a true proportion of the massacre. At the moment in the fight when he saw falling at his side strangers and friends, he looked at the casualties as something normal that inspired in him heroism and indignation. But now his eyes had gotten smaller or the death toll had mounted; his stare did not reach to cover them all, nor his mind to imagine such a quantity. A horrible pain entered him because those lives had been sacrificed uselessly. He surmised then the breadth of the betrayal. If the leaders who had said they represented the people had not allied with the unstable government, perhaps there would have been many more deaths, two or three times as many, but each one of them would have justified their sacrifice.

The magnitude of death and destruction is viewed here in

terms of betrayal and sacrifice. The unabated violent energy of the masses has not been channeled as a revolutionary force, but instead co-opted as an instrument of political compromise. Although the ending of *10th Street* is inconclusive, it is apparent that individual heroism and sacrifice are not enough. Such individual behavior should be the starting point for well-directed collective action.

Chambacú, a Black Ghetto

The opposite is true in the circumstances confronting Máximo, the resistance leader of the urban barrio of Chambacú who grounds his movement in history and myth. In *Chambacú, a Black Ghetto* the characters are just as hungry and oppressed as those in *10th Street*, but their outlook and sense of historical causality are different. Máximo interprets preliminary action in which the residents have thwarted an attempt to dislocate them in order to construct tourist hotels as a transformation from the traditional spiritual liberation of his ancestors to the physical dimension of the present. In assessing the present impact of past slavery and evangelization, he remarks:

Creen en la liberación por el milagro. Es la herencia de tantas bendiciones. Si alguien les habla de rebelarse, se asustan y persignan. Anoche gritaban, pero se acorbardaban en sus propios gritos. No creen que somos vigorosos y que unidos, seríamos capaces de construir murallas más fuertes que esas. Resistiríamos a cualquier ejército. Sin miedo y organizados, nos tragaríamos mil batallones.[11]

They believe in liberation by miracle. It is the heritage of so many blessings. If somebody talks to them about rebelling, they become frightened and annoyed. Last night they shouted but cowed at their own shouts. They do not believe that we are vigorous and that, united, we would be able to construct walls much stronger than those. We would resist any army. Without fear and organized, we would devour a thousand battalions.

The misery in Cartagena is as great as that in Bogotá, but the perceived solutions are different. While the disoriented masses of *10th Street* can only rely on political slogans, the protagonists of *Chambacú, a Black Ghetto* have centuries of history, toil, and struggle upon which to base their reaction. Only motivation and will are lacking, and this is provided with the death of Máximo, who projects a future in which "we would resist" and "we would devour" will be a concrete reality.

Chambacú, a Black Ghetto assesses life among Afro-Colombians in Chambacú, an isolated island/barrio of Cartagena, where the human fight for survival is of primary importance. The novel is divided into three sections: "Los reclutas" ("The Recruits"), "El botin" ("Booty"), and "La batalla" ("The Battle"), all three of which suggest warfare. Indeed, the motif of the Korean war provides the backdrop for the action in "The Recruits," the first section, as men are forcibly conscripted by the military to presumably serve in the national contingent in Korea. "Booty" is concerned with the war's aftermath and its impact on the barrio. Finally, "The Battle" deals with violent opposition to the idea of Chambacú's inhabitants being forced to move so that tourist facilities may be built and assesses their negative reaction to the Peace Corps.

The novel's focus is on the family of La Cotena, which consists of Máximo, a revolutionary; José Raquel, the manipulator; Clotilde, the daughter; Críspulo, a frustrated trainer of fighting cocks; and Medialuna, an undernourished punch-drunk prizefighter. José Raquel is captured, serves his military term, and returns with a new motorcycle and the Swedish woman Inge as booty. Máximo, however, refuses to go and spends several years in prison. As La Cotena hunts desperately for her sons the night of their capture, the words of Máximo are fresh in her memory:

Para mí no hay sino Chambacú. Ni siquiera Cartagena. Con lo mal que nos miran, ¿por qué ha de ir uno a pelear por ellos? Menos servir de burro de carga a los gringos. Si ellos quieren matar chinos y coreanos, será por que algo ganarán. Money. Es lo único que les interesa. Esos místeres tampoco saben lo que es democracia. Yo sé que allá cuelgan negros. Ahora quieren que nosotros les ayudemos a matar chinos. Buen negocio . . . (p. 37)

For me there is nothing but Chambacú. Not even Cartagena. Given the evil with which they look upon us, why does one have to fight for them? Not to mention serving as pack animals for the gringos. If they want to kill Chinese and Koreans, it will be because they will gain something. Money. It is the only thing that interests them. Those misters don't know what democracy is either. I know that over there they hang blacks. Now they want us to help them kill Chinese. Good business . . .

In this passage Máximo attacks United States imperialism, racism, and the hypocrisy of sending blacks to fight wars when they are subjected to abuses and treated as second-class citizens on their return. He articulates the same sentiments as Artel's and Palacios's protagonists concerning dependency and underdevelopment. Money, for Máximo, is truly the basis for all capitalistic evils. He refuses to be exploited for the purpose of making other people rich. In Chambacú, Máximo not only defies the authorities by painting revolutionary slogans on walls, but he also provides the impetus for rebellion.

Chambacú, a Black Ghetto assesses a crucial period in Colombian history, roughly 1952 through 1961. This was one of the most repressive and violent periods for the nation, immediately preceding the dictatorship of Rojas Pinilla. Zapata Olivella's treatment of the motif of the Korean war, which has such a negative impact on Chambacú, is based on facts. Colombia has the distinction of being the only South American country to commit troops for fighting alongside United States forces. A noted historian views the situation in the following manner:

El "hecho cumplido" del general Mac Arthur en Corea, dio a la dictadura colombiana la oportunidad de un pacto tenebroso con la Secretaria de Estado. A cambio de la complicidad de ésta, a cambio del silencio de las agencias noticiosas norteamericanas, a cambio de las armas que necesitaban para sofocar la creciente resistencia de los colombianos libres, la dictadura se apresuró a ofrecer y realizar el envío de tropas a Corea. Pasando por encima del precepto constitucional que exige la aprobación del Congreso para el envío de fuerzas armadas al exterior y contradiciendo la voluntad unánime de los colombianos, la dictadura tomó por su cuenta la iniciativa de incorporar soldados y marinos de nuestro ejército a las fuerzas expedicionarias enviadas a Corea.[12]

The "fait accompli" of General MacArthur in Korea gave the Colombian dictatorship the opportunity for a tenuous pact with the Secretary of State. In exchange for their complicity, in exchange for the silence of the North American news agencies, in exchange for arms necessary to suffocate the growing resistance by free Colombians, the dictatorship hurried to offer to send troops to Korea. Disregarding the constitutional amendment that requires the approval of Congress to send armed forces outside of the country and contradicting the unanimous will of Colombians, the dictatorship took upon itself the initiative of incorporating soldiers and marines of our army in the expeditionary forces sent to Korea.

During the dictatorship of Laureano Gómez, which ended in 1953, and the subsequent regime of Rojas Pinilla, Colombia's reputation as a country of violence was firmly established. As pointed out in the above passage, United States aid was obtained and used to repress Colombian citizens. Payment for arms and war materials was in the form of Colombian soldiers for Korea. These troops were sent against the dictates of the Constitution as well as against public opinion. What is important here are the self-serving interests of power that could not resist the opportunity to form a profitable pact with the United States government.

Chambacú, a Black Ghetto not only captures the spirit of resistance among a segment of the Afro-Colombian population but also shows the devastating effect of the war on inhabitants. For example, José Raquel displays a lack of morality by stealing and dealing in contraband, trades developed in Korea. War for him is truly "a good business." Many of Chambacú's inhabitants never return, but the mother of Atilio, who was machine-gunned, seems to have suffered the most. "La pobre enloquecio al recibir la noticia" (The poor thing went crazy upon receiving the news; p. 68). Later she fights actively to keep the Peace Corps out of Chambacú.

A period of violent social unrest provides the atmosphere for Zapata Olivella's interpretation of Colombian history during the fifties. His assessment is in keeping with historical interpretations of this period. On a more intimate level,

Zapata Olivella provides the reader with a glimpse at what was happening in the daily lives of Chambacú's inhabitants. We share their hunger, religious beliefs, frustrations, joys, medical insights, and all aspects of culture prevalent within the community. The sense of brotherhood in the face of adversity appears to be the key unifying element in Chambacú.

It is through Máximo that resistance to a system of internal colonization is manifested. Máximo's approach to the problem of liberation for Chambacú's population involves more than rhetoric. He operates from a strong historical and ideological frame of reference. This awareness is evident in his explanation of the Afro-Colombian situation to Inge.

Nuestra cultura ancestral también está ahogada. Se expresa en fórmulas mágicas. Supersticiones. Desde hace cuatrocientos años se nos ha prohibido decir "esto es mio." Nos expresamos en un idioma ajeno. Nuestros sentimientos no encuentran todavía las palabras exactas para afirmarse. Cuando me oyes hablar de revolución me refiero a algo más que romper ataduras. Reclamo el derecho simple de ser lo que somos. (p. 121)

Our ancestral culture is also strangled. It is expressed in magical formulas. Superstitions. For four hundred years we have been prohibited from saying "this is mine." We express ourselves in an alien tongue. Our feelings still do not find the exact words to affirm them. When you hear me speak of revolution I refer to something more than breaking shackles. I demand the simple right of being who we are.

For Máximo, rebellion means the recapturing of manhood lost during the dehumanizing process of slavery, which eliminated many positive aspects of culture. Part of the Afro-Colombian's being was stripped away, and self-affirmation is the only way to compensate for the loss. The attitude is evident in the statement "Reclamo el derecho simple de ser lo que somos" (I demand the simple right of being who we are). Positive values from the past will provide the inspiration for the present struggle.

Throughout the conversation with Inge, historical figures from Colombia's past such as Benkos Bioho and San Pedro

Claver are alluded to by Máximo in an effort to relate rebellious sentiments over the years. Máximo subsequently dies leading a demonstration against outside control of Chambacú. He and most of the residents will not tolerate being displaced in order to make room for the tourist industry, nor will they be pacified by the Peace Corps, which they view as an arm of Yankee imperialism. Máximo's death is not in vain because the seeds of rebellion have been sown and Chambacú inhabitants are prepared to fight against the soldiers and the corrupt officials. Richard L. Jackson has written, "Perhaps more than any other character in modern Latin American fiction, Máximo, in fact, is reminiscent of the revolutionary spirit that characterizes not only the black people in the United States today but civil rights activists in the Third World in general."[13] Máximo's speeches do have the ring of Black Power to them, and he is the catalyst for social action. Like Gregorio in *The Drenched Earth* and Jeremías in *In Chimá a Saint Is Born*, Máximo is willing to take risks in order to improve the plight of his people.

In the novels of Manuel Zapata Olivella that treat the Colombian milieu, rebellion is a community based, internal warfare. Although resistance and desire for change are inspired by social conditions, the type of guerrilla warfare advocated in *The Jungle and the Rain* and *It's Not Death, It's Dying* is not present in *The Drenched Earth*, *In Chimá a Saint Is Born*, and *Chambacú, a Black Ghetto*. Well-directed vertical violence, it is suggested, brings about better results than spontaneous self-destruction.

Behind the Mask

Behind the Mask has been the object of a great deal of critical activity. In his discussion of the development of the Colombian novel, Gerardo Suárez Rondón labels it "one of the most original novels, and perhaps one of the most interesting or important also within the thematics that we are studying."[14] Eduardo Camacho Guizado is not as positive: "The book supports itself in large part on the dramatics of an extraliterary situation, and its 'documentary' merit perhaps supersedes its purely novelistic value."[15] On the other hand,

Rubén Ruiz Camacho is very favorable: "We consider it the most magnificently accomplished novel of recent years. Never before, in the different attempts to fictionalize or dramatize facets of 'la violencia' has there been achieved an accuracy so fortunate as that found in *Behind the Mask*."[16]

This type of adulatory statement is very rare in the critical appraisal of Colombian literature. *Behind the Mask* did win the Esso Prize in 1962, which, according to Camacho Guizado, was at that time "the only novelistic reward of interest that the 'cultural country offers.'" Through a skillful fusion of form and content, Zapata Olivella has penned a work of high literary merit without compromising his basic thematic concerns with social change. The critics have managed to maintain the same type of ambivalence as the author's literary characters.

Some of the most naive criticism of *Behind the Mask* is found in an article by Julio Enrique Cuervo Escobar, who claims, "Zapata Olivella lacks, at least in *Behind the Mask*, more agility to move the characters and express ideas in dialogue." After failing to decipher the author's narrative technique, and multiperspectivism, Cuervo Escobar observes: "That is a 'defect' that shows us that more skill and more knowledge in the art of structuring the novel is lacking."[17]

Behind the Mask unifies many of Zapata Olivella's recurring themes from a psychological rather than a social realist perspective. It interprets aspects of both rural and urban existence—the violence of the Ibagué countryside and the sordid life of the urban *gamín* of Bogotá. The major advancement of *Behind the Mask* over the other early novels is in the realm of technique. In this work, Zapata Olivella uses a process of interiorization of experience instead of mere descriptions of series of occurrences. Many "new novel" techniques are incorporated, such as presenting an episode from multiple perspectives, flashbacks, as well as the use of letters and clinical documents as structural devices.

The central incident of *Behind the Mask* concerns the shooting of an anonymous street urchin who is subsequently identified as Jesús, Gil, Estanislao, and Ponciano. His photo in the paper provokes a number of responses from different sections of the country, although most of the action revolves around the Alcaidía de Menores, a home for delinquent minors, and the benign activities of Dr. Jáuregui. The central protagonist is supposed to have escaped from the hospital where he is confined at the end of *Behind the Mask*, ending the book on a mysterious note.

Behind the Mask concerns, on a higher plane, the relativity of truth and its alteration to satisfy individual needs. At the same time it presents the fallacy of trying to apply Freudian psychology to a set of inappropriate cultural circumstances. The rural ambience presented in this novel is related to that in *The Drenched Earth* and *In Chimá a Saint Is Born* in that banditry and political killings are much in evidence. The urban environment where gaining the mere necessities is a battle and where life is very cheap echoes the situations in *10th Street* and *Chambacú, a Black Ghetto*.

One of the keys to understanding *Behind the Mask* is a deciphering of its narrative structure. The novel is divided into two parts without any specific chapter designations. In the first ten pages, the reader is presented with half a dozen different perspectives on the death of the street urchin. The book begins with two anonymous thought segments, one in third person, the other in first; the focus then shifts to a third-person description of Otilia in school; then to a letter written by Octavio Guzmán; then to the reactions of Señora Ana Peñaranda; and then back to the narrator of the original first-person segment. Each of these perspectives pretends to offer insight into the background of the wounded youngster, whether he is Estanislao or Jesús at this point in the novel.

The first impression of the victim is presented from the perspective (we later determine) of Dr. Jáuregui, who is perusing the newspaper:

Una fotografía atrajo su atención, precisamente allí en la crónica roja. No era espeluznante como otras. La foto de un "gamín," un "pelafustán," como ahora llamaban desdeñosamente a un niño, a una vida promisoria, frustrada. Yacía tirado en la calle, contra un muro, encogido, como si durmiera. Su rostro le era conocido. Rememoró a los 220 niños recluidos en la Alcaidía de Menores. No era ninguno de los atendidos por él en esos días.[18]

A photograph attracted his attention, precisely there on the scandal sheet. It was not hair-raising like others. The photo of a "gamín," a "pelafustán," as now they called scornfully a child, a promising, frustrated life. He was lying stretched out in the street, against a wall, shriveled, as if asleep. His face was familiar. He remembered the 220 children shut up in the Alcaidía de Menores. He was not one of those cared for by him in those days.

This photograph and its story trigger an unprecedented response throughout various sectors of the country. The situation creates an ironic situation of multiple identities in a society that places minimum value on its young.

The first conflict surrounding the identity of the youth occurs when Ana Peñaranda enters the hospital with a priest to hear his confession.

> Octavio se sorprendió del interés de aquella señora por Estanislao. Miraba su aspecto de mujer capitalina, vestida de negro desde los zapatos hasta el sombrero. Nerviosa, intranquila, apretaba el misal contra su pecho.
> —Tuve que cerrar mi tiendecita para traer al reverendo padre. ¡Pobre Jesús no tiene a nadie en el mundo!
> Jáuregui miró de soslayo a Octavio, quien estaba cada vez más asombrado. Sin esconder su perplejidad el abogado la interrogó:
> —¿Decía usted que el niño se llama Jesús? (p. 35)

Octavio was surprised by the interest of that woman in Estanislao. He looked at her posture of a woman from the capital, dressed in black from head to toe. Nervous, unsettled, she clutched the missal to her breast.
"I had to close my little store to bring the blessed father. Poor Jesús does not have anybody in the world!"
Jáuregui looked askance at Octavio, who was even more astonished. Without hiding his perplexity the lawyer asked her: "Did you say the boy is named Jesús?"

Ana Peñaranda tells her own version of the truth, which opens the door for other versions of the story, especially when the patient in his delirium mentions the name of Otilia, daughter of the lawyer Octavio and his wife, Susana, from whose house Estanislao was supposed to have disappeared six years previously after allegedly sexually assaulting Otilia. The Guzmán family had taken in Estanislao after his family has been killed by rivals in Ibagué. From a psychological perspective this relationship raises the question of incest, oedipal considerations, and other Freudian commonplaces. The juxtaposing of past and present, of truth and lie, underscores the many ambiguities of *Behind the Mask*.

There remains a connection between Ana and the patient, whose name becomes Gil or Ponciano Peñaranda in the second part of the book. Also there is a great deal of emphasis placed on Freudian psychology, usually questioning the relationship between theory and practice. At times the attitude is sarcastic. Doctor Jáuregui is told:

Con sus palabras y consejos algo logra en las mentes asustadas de estos niños. Es mejor, doctor Jáuregui, que prosiga su pasatiempo de interpretaciones psicoanalíticas, soñando con la cleptomanía, el incesto y el homicidio como símbolos de afán de dominio u obsesiones compulsivas. Fantasee sobre mis aberraciones paranóicas, pero déjeme cumplir con mi deber de simple arconte. (p. 136)

With your words and advice something is achieved in the frightened minds of these children. It is better, Doctor Jáuregui, that you carry on your hobby of psychoanalytic interpretations, dreaming about kleptomania, incest, and homicide as symbols of the zeal to dominate or of compulsive obsessions. Fantasize about my paranoiac aberrations, but let me fulfill my duty as a simple therapist.

Behind the Mask is an essentially ironic novel that demonstrates the futility of trying to apply Freudian psychoanalytical methods to the violent world of the *gamín* and of adolescents in general, as demonstrated in the case of Otilia. Otilia and her mother have experienced a strained relationship since childhood, and it comes to a head with the appearance of Estanislao. The trauma of rape is foremost in Otilia's thoughts and actions throughout the episodes devoted to the Guzmán family, but finally the reader discovers that the entire experience has been structured around a lie. Otilia maintains: "Yo . . . , no he sido violada nunca por mi hermano. Porque no quiso jugar conmigo, yo misma me hice daño" (I . . . , have not ever been violated by my brother. Because he did not want to play with me, I harmed myself; p. 141).

The key to the unidentified *gamín's* identity is in the nature of the existence of such children. Otilia's mother consoles, "Esos niños que vagan por las calles, sometidos a la inclemencia y al hambre, acaban por parecerse" (Those children who roam the streets, subjected to bad weather and hunger, all look alike; p. 151). In *Behind the Mask* the thin line between appearance and reality, between truth and lie, is totally blurred in the multiplicity of interpretations of the central episode.

Changó, the Great SOB

Changó, the Great SOB is very different from the first series of novels by Zapata Olivella assessing the Colombian milieu. Although its main theme does scrutinize the transition from oppression to liberation among the black masses of the Americas, the movement occurs on a grand scale. The principal issue is the psychical and physical liberation of an entire ethnic group in its confrontation, as African prisoners, with Western culture. The inherent contrast in world views is one of the most traumatic conflicts encountered by the Africans in their transition to the Americas.

Changó, the Great SOB is divided into five parts: "Los Orígenes" ("Origins"), the African source; "El Muntu Americano" ("American Muntu"), the initial African confrontation with Colombian reality; "La Rebelión de los Vodus" ("The Voodoo Rebellion"), the Haitian revolutionary experience; "Las Sangres Encontradas" ("Meeting of the Bloods"), the black influence on revolutionary movements in South America and Mexico; and "Los Ancestros Combatientes" ("Battling Ancestors"), the struggle for freedom and equality in the United States. These collective experiences embrace nearly six centuries of societal confrontation and the quest for dignity. Changó, the Yoruba deity of war, fecundity, and dance—identified with the Catholic Santa Barbara—bears much of the responsibility for both positive and negative dimensions of the experiences narrated.

The keys to understanding *Changó, the Great SOB* include an appreciation of the African world view implicit in the novel as it relates to the concept of time and the dialectic between life and death. This novel examines slavery as the common denominator of black peoples throughout the Americas while at the same time bringing to the surface experiential images implicit in this experience. For example, "Los Ancestros"—the ancestral spirits from the African heritage—which are such an integral part of the narrative from the Middle Passage to Malcolm X, are, according to the approach to African time presented by Bonnie Barthold, "the intermediaries between the material world and the spiritual world who provide the means of protecting the present, guaranteeing the future and generally assuaging doubts and worries."[19] Birth and death are features of the same process, passage from the spirit world to the material world and vice versa.

Following the line of reasoning outlined by Barthold, in *Changó, the Great SOB* there is a movement from *synchrony*, or mythic and cyclic time, toward *diachrony*, history in which time is seen as a linear sequence. This is apparent in three stages: (1) cyclic time—myth—Africa; (2) the interval of passage—Africa/America—erosion of cyclicality, development of linearity; (3) linear time—history—America. In the experience of Afro-Americans, the interval of passage is the most traumatic, since there is a constant battle between the spiritual world of the ancestors and the process of zombification, or the conversion of Africans into deculturized work machines.

When Zapata Olivella was asked by Gilberto Gómez and Raymond Williams about the world view of *Changó, the Great SOB*, the following exchange occurred:

Q. Según lo que dices, ¿es posible afirmar que sea novela caribeña o novela africana? ¿Qué dirías?
A. Yo digo que es una nueva óptica de mirar la novela latinoamericana y yo diría que la cultura latino-americana, a la que estamos acostumbrados a ver desde el punto de vista del europeo, o del indio. Aunque se han escrito novelas con temática negra, no se ha intentado nunca una visión totalizadora de la cultural americana vista también desde el ángulo particular del negro, y esto es lo que pudiera darle una nueva caracterización esta novela. No se trata de una visión colombiana o india, ni de una visión europea, sino de la visión africana, pero no del africano puro que al llegar

conserva su cultura africana, sino del que se mezcla aquí en América, y cuya visión se enriquece con la visión del indio y la del blanco.[20]

Q. According to what you say, is it possible to affirm that the novel is Caribbean or African? What would you say?
A. I say that it is a new method of viewing the Latin American novel and I would say of Latin American culture, which we are accustomed to seeing from the European or Indian point of view. Although there have been novels written on black themes, there has never been attempted an all-encompassing vision of American culture seen also from the particular angle of the *negro*, and that is what could give a new characterization to this novel. It does not have to do with either a Colombian, an Indian, or a European vision, but with an African vision, not of the pure African who on arriving preserves his African culture, but with the one who mixes here in America, and whose vision is enriched with the vision of the Indian and of the white.

It is precisely this Afro-American conception of the universe, of biological *mestizaje* and cultural syncretism, incorporated into *Changó, the Great SOB*, that gives the novel its uniqueness as literature of the diaspora.

Changó, the Great SOB is the literary myth of the African dispersion throughout the Americas. In attempting to arrive at an Afro-American world view, the novel incorporates an African mythic conception of the origin of the universe with the subsequent movement of people. This approach is especially evident in the first part of the novel, where the narrative perspective is that of the African prisoners and how they must have perceived their circumstances. "Origins" elaborates, with a collective voice, the *intrahistoria* of the traffic in human flesh—the internal dynamics of the characters, relationships, betrayals, and cruelties. Consequently, the novel attempts to discover the positive dimension of capture, the middle passage, and rebellion, since the intent is to give life to the experience of imprisonment and exile. A single ship serves as a symbol and analogy for those that came before and after. By entering into African religious and other cultural myths and relating them to historical reality, Zapata Olivella presents a fictionalization of the plight of millions who were victims. Through its combination of history and legend, prose and poetry, "Origins" establishes the mythic basis of the narrative whose broad scope—embracing nations, peoples, great deeds, achievements, and failures—is maintained throughout.

The experience of imprisonment, exile, and resistance is repeated in the Spanish, French, and English contexts as Zapata Olivella explores this vast cultural intertext of the Americas. Cultural heroes such as Benkos Bioho, François Mackandal, and Nat Turner, to name a few, are given positive presentation in their push for liberation. The second part of *Changó, the Great SOB*, "American Muntu," which is devoted to the Colombian slavery experience, is concerned with the birth of Bioho and his emergence as the leader of El Palenque de San Basilio. His arrival is announced by one of the principal African *ancestros*:

—¡Oid, oídos del mundo. Oid! Aquí nace el vengador, ya está con nosotros el brazo de fuego, la muñeca que se escapará de los grillos, el diente que destroza las cadenas. ¡Oigan los que me oyen! Oigan ustedes que traen a esta vida los hijos del Muntu. Escuchen: el protegido de Elegba trae sangre de príncipe. Nace entre nosotros, será nuestro Rey. Protegido de Elegba será bautizado con el nombre cristiano de Domingo pero todos lo llamaremos Benkos, porque Benkos, se llama el tatarabuelo Rey que sembró su kulonda. Criado en la casa del padre Claver se alzará contra ella. Morirá en manos de sus enemigos pero su magara, soplo de otras vidas, revivirá en los ekobios que se alcen contra el amo.[21]

"Listen, ears of the world. Listen. Here the avenger is born, here with us is the firebrand, the wrist that will escape the shackles, the teeth that destroy chains. Hear those who listen to me. Hear you who bring into this life the children of the Muntu. Listen: the one protected by Elegba bears the blood of a prince. He is born among us, he will be our king. Protected by Elegba he will be baptized with the Christian name of Domingo, but all of us will call him Benkos, because Benkos is the name of the great great grandfather king who planted his umbilical cord. Raised in the house of St. Peter Claver he will rise up against her. He will die by the hands of his enemies but his soul, breath of other lives, shall live again in the blacks who rise up against the master."

From birth he is instilled with the values necessary to resist the dehumanizing practices of slavery. Bioho is a symbol of affirmation of humanity, that which the system attempts to negate. He is born under the sign of Elegba—intermediary between the dead and the living—with the image of serpents devouring themselves symbolically linking him to other liberators like Mackandal and Nat Turner.

Mackandal, the Haitian *cimarrón* who played such an important role in the liberation of that country, appears appropriately in the third section, "Voodoo Rebellion." Like Bioho, his presentation is a mixture of fact and fiction, which contributes to the mythic basis of the novel:

. . . Fue Mackandal el primero en convocar indios y negros contra la Loba Blanca. Antes que él, nadie pensó en ejércitos, generales, reyes, y emperadores negros . . . Con su brazo invisible ahorcó a los policías que lo llevan preso. Y sólo herido, acosado por los perros en un cafetal, puede aprisionarlo un ejército. (p. 178)

. . . Mackandal was the first to call together Indians and blacks against the White Wolf. Before him, nobody thought about black armies, generals, kings, and emperors . . . with his invisible arm he choked the policemen who took him prisoner. And alone and wounded, hunted down by dogs in a coffee field, the army can take him prisoner.

Later, Mackandal comments on his own burial:

Para que no hubiera duda riegan la ceniza de mi cadáver en la habitación de Dufrene donde estuve preso. Pero mis ekobios saben que convertido en la serpiente de Damballa renaceré triunfante en el arco iris después de cada tormenta. Soy el gallo que canta en las madrugadas. Por las noches con mis tropas me unía a los primeros jefes de la rebelión. (p. 180)

So that there can be no doubt, spread my ashes on the Dufrene place where I was held prisoner. But my black followers know that converted into the serpent of Damballa I will be reborn triumphantly in the rainbow after each storm. I am the cock who sings in the mornings. During the nights with my troops I joined the first leaders of the rebellion.

In the quest for psychical and physical liberation from the institution of slavery, it is apparent that the African world view is of the utmost importance. Mackandal burns at the stake, but in the minds of his followers he either flies away or assumes another life form. Thus, in their physical misery, they are able to escape to a mental world with positive models.

In the fifth section, "Battling Ancestors," Nat Turner takes a more direct, critical approach to the plight of the bondsmen. From the perspective of death in the nineteenth century, he addresses Agne Brown, a twentieth-century protagonist—thereby exemplifying the life/death dialectic between the *ancestros* and the living.

Comienzo por aclararte que mi rebelión no fue una rebelión. Estábamos y estamos en guerra a muerte contra el régimen esclavista que no conocía piedad ni ofrece cuartel al oprimido. Sufrir dieciocho y veinte horas de trabajo forzado es participar en una batalla donde los sobrevivientes son simples cadáveres desposeídos de alma, músculos y vida. Y desde luego para un esclavo todo amo, sea niño o adulto, es un opresor que solo nos alejará del trapiche cuando nos sepulte como un bagazo inútil. Así las cosas, Agne Brown, mi combate, la llamada rebelión de Nat Turner, solo era eso: Una batalla más en la gran guerra contra la esclavitud. (p. 392)

I begin by clarifying to you that my rebellion was not a rebellion. We were and are in a war to the death against the slavery regime, which knows no pity nor offers quarter to the oppressed. To suffer eighteen to twenty hours of forced labor is to participate in a battle where the survivors are merely corpses devoid of soul, muscles, and life. And also for a slave each owner, be he child or adult, is an oppressor who will only take us away from the mill when they bury us as useless waste. Thus things, Agne Brown, my battle, the so-called rebellion of Nat Turner, were only that: one more battle in the great war against slavery.

These three episodes, although separated by distance, nationality, time, and language, illustrate the same point. In spite of the oppression experienced by blacks, there was always the striving for liberation, a characteristic of the author's entire oeuvre. Out of this collective suffering, positive present-day models of resistance were born throughout the Americas.

In conclusion, *Changó, the Great SOB*, as a literary work spawned by the cultural intertext of slavery, can be viewed in terms of both its relationship to particular prior texts and its participation in the discursive space of Afro-American culture. An interesting analogy can be drawn, for instance, between the Mackandal episode in *The Kingdom of This World* by Alejo Carpentier and the more sophisticated presentation by Zapata Olivella. But more importantly, as Jonathan Culler points out, "The study of intertextuality is thus not the investigation of sources and influences as traditionally conceived; it casts its net wider to include anonymous discursive practices, codes whose origins are lost, that make possible the signifying practices of later texts."[22]

The greatest achievement of *Changó, the Great SOB* is to bring to the surface, from the African experience, these anonymous discursive practices and lost codes and to incorporate them into a literary experience assessing four centuries of black existence. The odyssey from Africa terminates with the death of Malcolm X, whose demise ends the novel on a revolutionary note. As Malcolm lies in state, Antonio Maceo, the Cuban general, passes his sword across Malcolm's lips and states: "—Ahora tus acciones guerreras—deben darle el filo que no tuvieron tus palabras" ("Now your warlike actions must give the edge that your words did not have"; p. 509) In the final analysis, action does speak louder than words.

Ian Smart has observed about *Changó, the Great SOB*,

It is Manuel Zapata Olivella's finest novel. It is the most substantial and perhaps the most important Afrocentric literary work in the Spanish language. It is a true American novel, since it tells the "historia toda de America" in a more complete manner than is possible within the narrow Eurocentric literary tradition.[23]

Changó, the Great SOB is the total novel of the Afro-American diaspora. It has the combination of myth and history, of truth and lie, that is necessary to the most enduring works of fiction.

In summary, from *The Drenched Earth* to *Chango, the Great SOB*, Manuel Zapata Olivella has created a *novelística*, that is, a body of high-quality novels interpreting the Colombian and American experiences. His works incorporate all of the thematic preoccupations that are so vital to Arnoldo Palacios, Carlos Arturo Truque, Jorge Artel, and Juan Zapata Olivella. Writing from the perspective of an Afro-Colombian, Manuel Zapata Olivella realizes that he has a dual responsibility: to his craft and to society.

6. Conclusion

The writers in this study do not represent a homogeneous group in background, outlook, or behavior. Their experiences as Colombians of African descent are different, and as such one could not expect them to produce a uniform body of literature interpreting the experiences of blacks in Colombia. The Zapata Olivellas have earned fame and recognition at home and abroad, while the importance of Artel as a national treasure is just being recognized. Conversely, Truque and Palacios led frustrating lives in Colombia—the former until his untimely death and the latter until his self-imposed exile.

These writers are from different geographic regions with different experiences and ways of viewing themselves and Colombia. Palacios and Truque are from the Chocó, Artel is from Cartagena, and the Zapata Olivellas are from Lorica. As one might expect, Palacios and Artel, from areas where there are suffering black majorities, are the most strident in their social condemnations, while Truque seeks a mastery of form over content. All these writers manage to portray destitute, desperate people without much hope. Consequently, their literary creations are different yet similar at the same time. Each in his own way expresses extreme disappointment with the plight of the poor in Colombia, with sentiments ranging from resignation to warfare. Therein lies their similarity. To emphasize this point, Richard Jackson has written, "Black literature opens windows to Latin American literature, but through a perspective seen 'from below' and 'from within.' This perspective is important and balances very well the better-known views 'from above.'"[1]

Many of the protagonists in the works of Arnoldo Palacios, Carlos Arturo Truque, Jorge Artel, Juan Zapata Olivella, and Manuel Zapata Olivella are more concerned with survival than with skin color or ethnic origins. As pointed out at the beginning of this study, *negritud* is not as much of a unifying concept in their work as is authenticity. How valid, then, is it to talk about Afro-Colombian prose fiction when, aside from one or two exceptions, the authors

Conclusion

do not dwell upon Afro-centric themes? If "Afro-Hispanic literature" means works by and about Afro-Hispanics exclusively, then my approach is not valid. However, if the term includes literature written by black Colombian writers who recognize that their ethnic background is important in formulating the manner in which they perceive themselves and their circumstances, then there is such a phenomenon. This has been my basic assumption throughout this study.

Thematically, this group of writers has much in common with the majority of Colombian authors and therefore follows past and current literary trends. Much literature has been written interpreting "La Violencia" in Colombia, and the interpretations of these five writers are not unique in treating the topic. What these writers do have to offer is a literary sensibility tempered by their experiences as blacks in Colombia. Perhaps some examples treating ideology and violence will help to illustrate this point.

In his article "Two Novelistic Views of the Bogotazo," Thomas E. Kooreman undertakes a comparative analysis of two novels treating the events of 9 April 1948 relating to the assassination of Gaitán and the destruction of Bogotá. The works are *El monstruo* by Carlos H. Pareja and *La calle 10* by Manuel Zapata Olivella. In his concluding remarks Kooreman notes:

> The historical moment of the *bogotazo*, emphasizing the same socio-political themes, is as obvious in *La calle 10* as it is in *El monstruo*. Although the latter work offers the interested reader a step by step account of the tragedy, it must be observed that the author's very emphasis on exposing the political forces in play by name tends to reduce its artistic value. On the other hand, *La calle 10* presents the same social message more effectively through the artistic use of universal circumstances integrated with appropriate structural and narrative techniques.[2]

On balance, Zapata Olivella is a better novelist than Pareja, so we would expect him to have a superior command of narrative technique. But this observation by Kooreman also reiterates the observation by Richard Jackson cited at the beginning of this study that, when interpreting the plight of the masses, Afro-Hispanic writers are much more adept than their well-meaning *criollo* counterparts. Zapata Olivella is able to capture the human experiences associated with the *bogotazo* from an insider's perspective rather than from the distant posture assumed by Pareja. As a result, his novel is a much more accomplished work of fiction depicting a human tragedy.

Another comparison will illustrate how the Afro-Colombian writer handles the responsibility of interpreting the plight of the masses. Jorge Artel's interpretation of "La Violencia" is in the same literary mode as such works as *Lo que el cielo no perdona, novela histórica* (*What Heaven Does Not Pardon, a Historical Novel*, 1954) by Ernesto León Herrera, *El Cristo de espaldas* (*Christ Turns His Back*, 1953) by Eduardo Caballero Calderón, *La mala hora* (*In Evil Hour*, 1962) by Gabriel García Márquez, and *El día señalado* (*On the Appointed Day*, 1964) by Manuel Mejía Vallejo.[3] The basic difference between Artel's novel and those of the other four authors is the method offered for improving the plight of the oppressed.

In this regard, the role of the Catholic Church in the unmitigated historical violence that has occurred in Colombia is another literary aspect to consider. In the aforementioned novels by León Herrera and Caballero Calderón, the priests empathize with the poor and become introspective rebels of conscience. In the novels of García Márquez and Mejía Vallejo, the Church's representatives remain aloof and insensitive to the plight of the rebels. On the other hand, Jorge Artel uses Camilo Torres, a contemporary martyr, to call for revolution and the implementation of Liberation Theology as a solution.

In the prose fiction of Afro-Colombian writers, the trend is to go beyond official religion and to have protagonists take matters into their own hands. Witness the situations in *The Jungle and the Rain*, *In Chimá a Saint Is Born*, and *It's Not Death, It's Dying*. Palacios, Artel, Truque, and the Zapata Olivellas all view the Church, the military, and the oligarchy as being in complicity. As writers who understand the plight of the masses, they subsequently resist the status quo, realizing that there will be no fundamental changes in Colombian

Conclusion

society unless the Catholic Church dares to take the initiative.

These two examples also illustrate that Afro-Colombian writers are cognizant of and well within national literary trends. To approach their literary craft any differently would result in even more of a distance between themselves and their audience, since the people about whom they write are not likely to read their works. Social protest and calls for change must be within clearly defined literary norms.

In the closing comments of her discussion of "Trends and Priorities for Research on Latin American Literature," Jean Franco observes: "the overall trend in the 1980's is towards the development of sociocriticism. This extends our capacity to understand how literary and non-literary texts construct social meanings and how they manage heterogeneous elements and position readers by the very process of textual organization."[4] Approaches to Afro-Colombian literature must take into account the types of form and content relationships alluded to here. This literature should also be viewed as an expression of the society of which it forms a part and not merely as an exercise in creative writing. Studying the role of the reader, discourse analysis, advanced formalism, as well as other approaches should be utilized to determine how "texts construct social meanings." This is the major concern of Afro-Colombian prose fiction writers.

Notes

Notes to Chapter 1. Introduction

1. Edward Kamau Brathwaite, "The African Presence in Caribbean Literature."
2. Richard L. Jackson, "Literary Blackness and Literary Americanism: Toward an Afro-Model for Latin American Literature," p. 7.
3. Ibid., p. 8.
4. Max Dorsinville, "Senghor or the Song of Exile," in Rowland Smith, ed., *Exile and Tradition: Studies in African and Caribbean Literature*, p. 67.
5. Paul Ilie, *Literature and Inner Exile*, p. 6.
6. Jonathan Culler, *The Pursuit of Signs: Semiotics, Literature, Deconstruction*, p. 103.
7. Terry Eagleton, *Marxism and Literary Criticism*, pp. 16-17.
8. Raymond Williams, *Marxism and Literature*, p. 55.
9. Raymond Williams, *The Sociology of Culture*, p. 26.
10. Catherine Belsey, *Critical Practice*, pp. 56–57.
11. Ibid., p. 61.
12. There is still a great deal of disagreement concerning the death of Gaitán and the subsequent Colombian reaction. "The assassin of Gaitán worked in combination with another accomplice" read a recent headline in *El Tiempo* (22 June 1986, p. 8B) that preceeded a discussion of the latest theories of Rafael Golán Medellín, who presents several versions of the act itself. The most thorough investigation of Gaitán and his era is *The Assassination of Gaitán: Public Life and Urban Violence in Colombia* by Herbert Braun, who treats this episode in Colombia history, with sophistication, as a riot.
13. Ariel Dorfman, *Imaginación y violencia en América*, p. 11. "La violencia en la novela hispanoamericana actual," pp. 9–37, is the essay that presents most of his basic ideas. In his recent study, *García Márquez y la novela de la violencia en Colombia*, Manuel Antonio Arango makes some pertinent observations:

Cuando la violencia tiene orígenes en un subdesarrollo, condición que conlleva a la miseria, la injusticia, el despojo, el coloniaje y el racismo crea una literatura de violencia como consecuencia histórica. Así los escritores que se agrupan bajo el término de novelistas de la 'Violencia' en Colombia, señalan las más bárbaras de las violencias: la violencia contra la masa campesina y contra los pueblos. Es en el fondo, una violencia de subdesarrollo, primitiva, bárbara e infrahumana. (p. 18)

When violence has its origins in underdevelopment, a condition that carries with it misery, injustice, pillage, colonialism, and racism creates a literature of violence as a historical consequence. Thus the writers who are grouped under the term novelists of "violence" in Colombia point out the most barbarous of the violent tendencies: violence against rural masses and towns. It is in essence, a violence of underdevelopment, primitive, barbarous, and infrahuman.

It is worth noting also that the topic of a recent meeting of the Association of North American Colombianists was "The Violence of Colombia." This event took place at Cornell University, 22-25 April 1987.

14. Dorfman, *Imaginación y violencia*, pp. 17, 23.

15. Another important study of violence is Julio Ortega and Cecilia Bustamante, "Para una tipología de la violencia." They outline five types of violence: historical, structural, repressive, institutional, and noncommunicative. Of the five categories, structural and institutional violence are those that impact most severely on the protagonists of Afro-Colombian writers. That is not to say that other forms of violence are not present in their literary worlds.

16. Barry D. Amis, "The Negro in the Colombian Novel," and Carl Erol Pedersen, Jr., "Main Trends in the Contemporary Colombian Novel, 1953-1967."

17. Nestor Madrid-Malo, "Estado actual de la novela en Colombia," p. 81. Other standard studies of the Colombian novel include Eduardo Pachón Padilla, "Panorama de la novela colombiana en el siglo XX," and Eduardo Camacho Guizado, "Novela colombiana: panorama contemporáneo." Recent book-length evaluations of Colombian prose fiction include two solid studies: Seymour Menton, *La novela colombiana: planetas y satélites*, and Raymond L. Williams, *Una década de la novela colombiana: la experiencia de los setenta*.

Notes to Chapter 2. Colombian Hunger: Arnoldo Palacios

1. Nina S. de Friedemann, "Negros en Colombia: Invisibilidad y Presencia," in Zapata Olivella, Manuel, ed., *El Negro en la historia de Colombia: Fuentes escritas y orales*, p. 88.

2. John S. Brushwood, *The Spanish American Novel: A Twentieth Century Survey*, pp. 156-79.

3. Raymond Williams, *Marxism and Literature*, p. 55.

4. Alvaro Monroy, "Un Admirable Esfuerzo: Arnoldo Palacios," p. 6.

5. Vicente Pérez Silva, review of *Las estrellas son negras*, p. 19.

6. Humberto Bronx, *20 años de novela colombiana*, p. 20.

7. Lillian R. Furst and Peter N. Skrine. *Naturalism*, pp. 42-43.

8. Arnoldo Palacios. *Las estrellas son negras*, 1949 (Bogotá: Edi-

torial Revista Colombiana, 1971), pp. 27-28. Further citations will be made parenthetically in the text.
  9. Furst and Skrine, *Naturalism*, p. 16.
  10. J.M.D., "La segunda novela de Arnoldo Palacios," p. 45.
  11. Arnoldo Palacios, *La selva y la lluvia* (Moscow: Ediciones en Lenguas Estranjeras, 1958), p. 46. Further citations will be made parenthetically in the text.
  12. Aquiles Escalante, *La minería del hambre: Condoto y la Chocó Pacífico*, p. 121.
  13. Terry Eagleton, *Marxism and Literary Criticism*, p. 6.

Notes to Chapter 3. The Literary Synthesizer: Carlos Arturo Truque

  1. Margaret Sayers Peden, ed., *The Latin American Short Story: A Critical History*.
  2. Enrique Pupo Walker, ed., *El cuento hispanoamericano ante la crítica*.
  3. Luis Leal, *Historia del cuento hispanoamericano*, 2d ed., p. 152. In a recent discussion of the short story in Colombia titled "El nuevo cuento colombiano," Eduardo Pachón Padilla refers to Truque, "con sus problemas del proletariado, tanto los de la zona rural como la urbana, a través de sus repercusiones en un medio reverberado por el calor, el sexo y la miseria" (with his problems of the proletariat, as much from the rural zone as from the urban, through their repercussions in an environment pulsating with heat, sex and misery; p. 885).
  4. Gustavo Alvarez Gardeazábal, "The Short Story in Colombia," p. 71.
  5. J. M. Alvarez D'Orsonville, "Two Interviews," pp. 92-93. Truque's assessment of the development of the Colombian short story is included in his "El cuento: una narración en desarrollo."
  6. Ibid., pp. 95-96.
  7. The difficulties associated with arriving at a coherent definition of the short story as a genre have been articulated recently by Valerie Shaw in *The Short Story: A Critical Introduction*, pp. 1-29 and by Ian Reid in *The Short Story*, pp. 1-14.
  8. George McMurray, "The Spanish American Short Story from Borges to the Present," in Peden, ed., *The Latin American Short Story*, p. 105.
  9. Carlos Arturo Truque, "La vocación y el medio: historia de un escritor," 484.
  10. Ibid., p. 485.
  11. Carlos Arturo Truque, *Granizada y otros cuentos* (Bogotá: Ediciones Espiral, 1953), p. 7. Further citations will be made parenthetically in the text.
  12. McMurray, *Latin American Short Story*, p. 115.

13. Carlos Arturo Truque, *El día que terminó el verano y otros cuentos* (Bogotá: Instituto Colombiano de Cultura, 1973), p. 12. Further citations will be made parenthetically in the text.

14. These ideas are contained in chap. 4 of *A Handbook of Critical Approaches to Literature* by Wilfred L. Guerin, et al., pp. 115-150.

15. Isabel Aretz, "Música y danza (América Latina continental, excepto Brasil)," in *Africa en América Latina*, ed. Manuel Moreno Fraginals, p. 260.

Notes to Chapter 4. The Poet as Novelist: Jorge Artel and Juan Zapata Olivella

1. Stanislaw Eile, "The Novel as an Expression of the Writer's Vision of the World," p. 115.

2. Terry Eagleton, *Marxism and Literary Criticism*, p. 6.

3. Jorge Artel, *No es la muerte, es el morir* . . . (Bogotá: ECOE Ediciones, 1979), p. 15. Further citations will be made parenthetically in the text. A discussion of the portrayal of the guerrilla movement in Colombian literature during the last fifteen years is found in "Guérillas et guérilléros dans le récit colombien actuel" by Jacques Gilard. He does not mention Jorge Artel. Herbert Braun, the historian, notes: "Gaitán wanted to represent the *pueblo*. He was the first politician to speak directly to the majority of Colombians. He spoke their language, came from their ranks. He needed the *pueblo* to have any chance in the *país político*. In that unequal reciprocity lie the uncertain seeds of democracy. A Gaitán government would have been a government of the emerging middle sector groups, of the petit bourgeoisie claiming to represent the *pueblo*. It was only through such a broad coalition, carried through in the long-established, multiclass parties of the nation, that Gaitán's own small class might exert its influence in society. In that class alliance, those within the *pueblo* who did not own property, workers and peasants, stood much to gain" (*The Assassination of Gaitán: Public Life and Urban Violence in Colombia*, p. 204).

4. His attempts to make peace with the two most important guerrilla groups, the April 19 Movement and the Colombian Revolutionary Armed Forces, proved unsuccessful. Cease fires to end the modern violence, which has been going on since the early 1960s, have been signed and violated. The most recent example of this destructive tendency occurred in November 1985 when guerrilla forces occupied the Palace of Justice and were expelled by the army, resulting in the loss of more than one hundred lives.

5. Penny Lernoux, *Cry of the People*, p. 31.

6. Jorge Artel, *Poemas con botas y banderas*, p. 23.

7. Ibid., p. 26.

8. Ibid., pp. 33-34.

9. Jorge Artel, *Antología poética*, pp. 30-31.

10. Juan Zapata Olivella, *Historia de un joven negro* (Port-au-Prince: Edición Haitiana Le Natal, 1983), p. 181. Further citations will be made parenthetically in the text.
11. Carlos Bousoño, *Epocas literarias y evolución: edad media, romanticismo, época contemporánea*, pp. 39-40.
12. Linda Hutcheon, *A Theory of Parody: The Teachings of Twentieth Century Art Forms*, pp. 32, 6.
13. This description is repeated at the beginning of the beauty contest activities: "Era una diafana mañana cuando la bahía resplandecía como un diamante" (It was a diaphanous morning when the bay glittered like a diamond; p. 88).
14. Bousoño, *Epocas literarias*, p. 42.
15. Juan Zapata Olivella, *Pisando el camino de ébano* (Bogotá: Ediciones Lerner, 1984), p. 3. Further citations will be made parenthetically in the text.

Notes to Chapter 5. From Oppression to Liberation: Manuel Zapata Olivella

1. This chapter is an expanded version of "La trayectoria novelística de Manuel Zapata Olivella: De la opresión a la liberación," which appeared in *Ensayos de literatura Colombiana*, ed. Raymond L. Williams, pp. 137-48. Manuel Zapata Olivella's latest novel, *El fusilamiento del diablo* (*The Execution of the Devil*, 1986), is an interpretation of the life and times of Manuel Saturio Valencia, a black man who was shot by a firing squad in Quibdó in 1907 for the crime of arson. Valencia was, supposedly, the last person executed under Colombia's capital punishment law. In 1953, Rogerio Velásquez, the black Colombian anthropologist, had published *Las memorias del odio* (*Memories of Hate*), a fictional biography of Valencia, which is very similar to the novel by Manuel Zapata Olivella. Whereas *Memories of Hate* is presented in straightforward narrative discourse—from Valencia's own recollections, official documents, and the testimony of individuals—*The Execution of the Devil* incorporates a variety of literary techniques to capture the multifaceted nature of black Chocoan existence. *The Execution of the Devil* continues the trends of violence and resistance that are characteristic of the novels of Manuel Zapata Olivella.
2. Francisco José González, "*Tierra mojada*."
3. Gloria Durán Salcedo, "Aspectos costumbristas en *Tierra mojada*, novela de Manuel Zapata Olivella."
4. Ibid., p. 30.
5. Manuel Zapata Olivella, *Tierra mojada*, 1947 (Medellín: Editorial Bedout, 1978), p. 23. Further citations will be made parenthetically in the text.
6. Manuel Zapata Olivella, *En Chimá nace un santo* (Barcelona: Seix Barral, 1964), p. 58. Further citations will be made parenthetically in the text.

7. Agustín Rodríguez, review of *La calle 10*.
8. Wanda Caruso, "*La calle 10*," paper presented for the Seminario Andrés Bello, pp. 42, 44.
9. John S. Brushwood, *The Spanish American Novel: A Twentieth Century Survey*, p. 227.
10. Manuel Zapata Olivella, *La calle 10* (Bogotá: Ediciones Casa de la Cultura, 1960), p. 10. Further citations will be made parenthetically in the text.
11. Manuel Zapata Olivella, *Chambacú, corral de negros*, 1963 (Medellín: Editorial Bedout, 1978), p. 123. Further citations will be made parenthetically in the text.
12. Diego Montana Cuéllar, *Colombia: País formal y país real*, p. 202.
13. Richard L. Jackson, *The Black Image in Latin American Literature*, p. 120. In the same vein, Leslie B. Rout, Jr., notes, "A hopeful Manuel Zapata Olivella proposed an amorphous form of biracial solidarity in *Corral de negros*. The question is never whether prejudice exists because this is an accepted fact. In Zapata Olivella's eyes, the racist Colombian oligarchs are merely lackeys of that great racist oppressor, the United States of America. Seemingly, his final solution is to smash the power of the Yankee imperialists with a Marxist-oriented, Third World coalition of like-minded (and/or darkskinned) souls" (*The African Experience in Spanish America*, p. 249).
14. Gerardo Suárez Rondón, *La novela sobre la violencia en Colombia*, pp. 37-38.
15. Eduardo Camacho Guizado, review of *Detrás del rostro*, p. 2019.
16. Rubén Ruiz Camacho, "*Detrás del rostro*, una novela ejemplar," p. 105.
17. Julio Enrique Cuervo Escobar, "*Detrás del rostro*: una acusación a la sociedad," pp. 17, 32.
18. Manuel Zapata Olivella, *Detrás del rostro* (Madrid: Aguilar, 1963), p. 18. Further citations will be made parenthetically in the text.
19. Bonnie J. Barthold. *Black Time: Fiction of Africa, the Caribbean and the United States*, pp. 31-49.
20. Raymond L. Williams and Gilberto Gómez, "Interview with Manuel Zapata Olivella," p. 657.
21. Manuel Zapata Olivella, *Changó, el gran putas*, pp. 97-98. Further citations will be made parenthetically in the text.
22. Jonathan Culler, *The Pursuit of Signs: Semiotics, Literature, Deconstruction*, p. 103.
23. Ian Smart, review of *Changó, el gran putas*, p. 32.

Notes to Chapter 6. Conclusion

1. Richard L. Jackson, "The Human Legacy of Black Latin American Literature," pp. 157-158.
2. Thomas E. Kooreman, "Two Novelistic Views of the Bogotazo," p. 135.

3. A discussion of these novels is found in Robert Kirsner, "Four Colombian Novels of 'La Violencia.'"

4. Jean Franco, "Trends and Priorities for Research on Latin American Literature," p. 118.

Bibliography

General

Abrams, M. H. *The Mirror and the Lamp: Romantic Theory and the Critical Tradition.* New York: Oxford University Press, 1953.
Afro-Hispanic Review. 5 vols., *1982, 1983, 1984, 1985, 1986.* Washington: Afro-Hispanic Institute, 1982–.
Barthold, Bonnie. *Black Time: Fiction of Africa, the Caribbean and the United States.* New Haven: Yale University Press, 1981.
Belsey, Catherine. *Critical Practice.* New York: Methuen, 1980.
Bousoño, Carlos. *Epocas literarias y evolución: edad media, romanticismo, época contemporánea.* Madrid: Editorial Gredos, 1981.
Brathwaite, Edward. "The African Presence in Caribbean Literature." *Daedalus* 103:2 (1974):73–109.
Brookshaw, Michael. "Protest, Militancy, and Revolution: The Evolution of the Afro-Hispanic Novel of the Diaspora." Ph.D. dissertation, University of Illinois, 1983.
Brotherston, Gordon. *The Emergence of the Latin American Novel.* New York: Cambridge University Press, 1977.
Brushwood, John S. *The Spanish American Novel: A Twentieth Century Survey.* Austin: University of Texas Press, 1975.
Cuéllar, Diego Montana. *Colombia: país formal y país real.* Buenos Aires: Editorial Platina, 1963.
Culler, Jonathan. *The Pursuit of Signs: Semiotics, Literature, Deconstruction.* Ithaca: Cornell University Press, 1981.
DeCosta, Miriam. "The Use of African Folklore in Hispanic Literature." *Caribbean Quarterly* 23:1 (1977):22–30.
Dorfman, Ariel. *Imaginación y violencia en America.* Santiago de Chile: Editorial Universitaria, 1970.
Eagleton, Terry. *Literary Theory: An Introduction.* Minneapolis: University of Minnesota Press, 1983.
———. *Marxism and Literary Criticism.* Berkeley: University of California Press, 1976.
Eile, Stanislaw. "The Novel as an Expression of the Writer's Vision of the World." *New Literary History* 9:1 (1977):115-28.
Franco, Jean. "Trends and Priorities for Research on Latin American Literature." *Ideologies and Literatures* 4:16 (1983):107–20.
Furst, Lilian R., and Skrine, Peter N. *Naturalism.* London: Methuen, 1971.
Glowinski, Michal. "On the First Person Novel." *New Literary History* 9:1 (1977):103–13.
González Echevarría, Roberto, ed. *Historia y ficción en la narrativa hispanoamericania: coloquio de Yale.* Caracas: Monte Avila, 1984.

Guerin, Wilfred, et al. *A Handbook of Critical Approaches to Literature.* New York: Harper and Row, 1966.
Hawkes, Terence. *Structuralism and Semiotics.* Berkeley: University of California Press, 1977.
Hutcheon, Linda. *A Theory of Parody: The Teachings of Twentieth Century Art Forms.* New York: Methuen, 1985.
Ilie, Paul. *Literature and Inner Exile.* Baltimore: Johns Hopkins University Press, 1980.
Jackson, Richard L. *The Afro-Spanish American Author: An Annotated Bibliography of Criticism.* New York: Garland Publishing, 1980.
―――. *The Black Image in Latin American Literature.* Albuquerque: University of New Mexico Press, 1976.
―――. *Black Writers in Latin America.* Albuquerque: University of New Mexico Press, 1979.
―――. "The Human Legacy of Black Latin American Literature." *CLA Journal* 30:2 (1986):154-70.
―――. "Literary Blackness and Literary Americanism: Toward an Afro-Model for Latin American Literature." *Afro-Hispanic Review* 1:2 (1982):5-11.
Jackson, Shirley. *La novela negrista en hispanoamerica.* Madrid: Editorial Piliegos, 1986.
Johnson, Lemuel. "Cross and Consciousness: The Failure of Orthodoxy in Black Diaspora Literature." In *Studies in Afro-Hispanic Literature, Vol. II-III, 1978-1979*, pp. 53-89. New York: Medgar Evers College, 1980.
Kubayanda, Josaphat Bekunuru. "Afrocentric Hermeneutics and the Rhetoric of 'Transculturación' in Black Latin American Literature." *Proceedings of the October 1983 Conference of the Canadian Association for Latin American Studies*, Ottowa, Canada (1984):226-40.
Leal, Luis. *Historia del cuento hispanoamericano.* 2d ed. Mexico: Ediciones de Andrea, 1971.
Lernoux, Penny. *Cry of the People.* New York: Penguin Books, 1980.
Lowe, Elizabeth. "Visions of Violence: From Faulkner to the Contemporary City Fiction of Brazil and Colombia." *Proceedings of the Xth Congress of the International Comparative Literature Association* (1982):14-19.
Luis, William, ed. *Voices from Under: Essays on Black Narrative in Latin America and the Caribbean.* Westport: Greenwood Press, 1984.
Mbiti, John S. *African Religions and Philosophy.* New York: Praeger Publishers, 1969.
Moreno Fraginals, Manuel, ed. *Africa en América Latina.* Mexico City: Siglo XXI, 1977.
Ortega, Julio, and Cecilia Bustamante. "Para una tipología de la violencia." *Eco* 232 (1981):395-407.

Palmer, Richard E. *Hermeneutics*. Evanston: Northwestern University Press, 1969.
Peden, Margaret Sayers, ed. *The Latin American Short Story: A Critical History*. Boston: Twayne Publishers, 1983.
Piedra, José. "Literary Whiteness and the Afro-Hispanic Difference." *New Literary History* 18:2 (1987):303-32.
Pupo Walker, Enrique, ed. *El cuento hispanoamericano ante la crítica*. Madrid: Castalia, 1973.
Reid, Ian. *The Short Story*. London: Methuen, 1977.
Rout, Leslie B. *The African Experience in Spanish America*. New York: Cambridge University Press, 1976.
Schwartz, Kessel. *A New History of Spanish American Fiction*. 2 vols. Coral Gables: University of Miami Press, 1972.
Shaw, Donald. *Nueva narrativa hispanoamericana*. Madrid: Ediciones Cátedra, 1981.
Shaw, Valerie. *The Short Story: A Critical Introduction*. New York: Longman, 1983.
Smith, Rowland. *Exile and Tradition: Studies in African and Caribbean Literature*. New York: Holmes and Meier, 1976.
Studies in Afro-Hispanic Literature. 3 vols., *1977, 1978, 1979*. New York: Medgar Evers College, 1980.
Studies in Short Fiction 8:1 (1971), volume devoted to the Latin-American short story.
Vidal, Hernan. *Sentido y prática de la crítica literaria sociohistórica: panfleto para la proposición de una arqueología acotada*. Minneapolis: Institute for the Study of Ideologies and Literatures, 1984.
White, Hayden. *Tropics of Discourse: Essays in Cultural Criticism*. Baltimore: Johns Hopkins University Press, 1978.
Williams, Raymond. *Marxism and Literature*. Oxford: Oxford University Press, 1977.
———. *The Sociology of Culture*. New York: Schocken Books, 1982.

Colombia

Amis, Barry D. "The Negro in the Colombian Novel." Ph.D. dissertation, Michigan State University, 1970.
Arango, Manuel Antonio. *Gabriel García Márquez y la novela de la violencia en Colombia*. Mexico City: Fondo de Cultura Económica, 1985.
Ayala Poveda, Fernando. *Manual de literatura colombiana*. Bogotá: Educar Editores, 1984.
Ayala Poveda, Fernando. *Novelistas colombianos contemporáneos*. Bogotá: Universidad Central, N.D.

Braun, Herbert. *The Assassination of Gaitán: Public Life and Urban Violence in Colombia*. Madison: University of Wisconsin Press, 1985.

Bronx, Humberto. *20 años de novela colombiana*. Medellín: Editorial Granamericana, 1966.

Camacho Guizado, Eduardo. "Novela colombiana: panorama contemporáneo." *Letras Nacionales* 9 (1966):18–37.

Carrillo, German. "La narrativa colombiana (1960–70)." *Nueva Narrativa Hispanoamericana* 2:1 (1972):149–57.

Castillo Muñoz, Juan. "Perspectivas de la literatura colombiana." *Boletín Cultural y Bibliográfico* 19:4 (1982):107–13.

Curcio Altamar, Antonio. *Evolución de la novela colombiana*. Bogotá: Instituto Caro y Cuervo, 1957.

de Friedemann, Nina S., and Rosselli, Carlos Patino. *Lengua y sociedad en el Palenque de San Basilio*. Bogotá: Instituto Caro y Cuervo, 1983.

Escalante, Aquiles. *La minería del hambre: Condoto y la Chocó Pacífico*. Barranquilla: Editorial Mejoras, 1971.

Gardeazábal, Gustavo Alvarez. "The Short Story in Colombia." *Review* 3 (1970):70–72.

Gerdes, Dick. "*Estaba la pájara sentada en el verde limón*: novela testimonial/documental de 'la violencia' en Colombia." *Revista de Estudios Colombianos* 2 (1987):21–26.

Gilard, Jacques. "Guérillas et guérilléros dans le récit colombien actuel." *Cahiers Du Monde Hispanique et Luso-Bresilien* 42 (1984):61–76.

Gutiérrez Azopardo, Ildefonso. *Historia del negro en Colombia*. Bogotá: Editorial Nueva America, 1980.

Kirsner, Robert. "Four Colombian Novels of 'La Violencia.'" *Hispania* 49:1 (1966):70–74.

Kooreman, Thomas E. "Two Novelistic Views of the Bogotazo." *Latin American Literary Review* 3:5 (1974):131–35.

López Tames, Ramón. *La narrativa actual de Colombia y su contexto social*. Valladolid: Universidad de Valladolid, 1975.

Madrid-Malo, Nestor. "Estado actual de la novela en Colombia." *Revista Interamericana de Bibliografía* 17:1 (1967):68–82.

Menton, Seymour. *La novela colombiana: planetas y satélites*. Bogotá: Plaza y Janes, 1978.

Pachón Padilla, Eduardo. "El nuevo cuento colombiano—Generación de 1970: nacidos de 1940 a 1954." *Revista Iberoamericana* 50:128–29 (1984):883–901.

———. "Panorama de la novela colombiana en el siglo XX." *Letras Nacionales* 30 (1976):5–39.

Pedersen, Carl Erol. "Main Trends in the Contemporary Colombian Novel, 1953–1967." Ph.D. dissertation, University of Southern California, 1971.

Pfeiffer, Erna. *Literarische Struktur und Realitatsbezug in kolumbianischen Violencia-Roman*. New York: Peter Lang, 1984.
Prescott, Laurence. *Candelario Obeso y la iniciación de la poesía negra en Colombia*. Bogotá: Instituto Caro y Cuervo, 1985.
Sánchez López, Luis María. *Diccionario de escritores colombianos*. Bogotá: Plaza y Janes, 1982.
Santa, Eduardo. *¿Qué Pasó el 9 de Abril?* Bogotá: Ediciones Tercer Mundo, 1982.
Suárez Rondón, Gerardo. *La novela sobre la violencia en Colombia*. Bogotá: Luis F. Serrano, 1966.
Velásquez, Rogerio. *El Chocó en la independencia de Colombia*. Bogotá: Editorial Hispana, 1965.
———. *Las memorias del odio*. Bogotá: Alianza de Escritores Colombianos, 1953.
Williams, Raymond L. *Una década de la novela colombiana: la experiencia de los setenta*. Bogotá: Plaza y Janes, 1981.
———. *La novela colombiana contemporánea*. Bogotá: Plaza y Janes, 1976.
———. "La novela colombiana 1960-1974: una bibliografía." *Chásqui* 5:3 (1976):27-39.
Williams, Raymond L., ed. *Ensayos de literatura colombiana*. Bogotá: Plaza y Janes, 1985.
Zapata Olivella, Manuel, ed. *El negro en la historia de Colombia: fuentes escritas y orales*. Bogotá: Fondo Interamericano de Publicaciones de la Cultura Negra, 1985.

Authors

Jorge Artel

Work Discussed
No es la muerte, es el morir . . . Bogotá: ECOE Ediciones, 1979.

Other Works Consulted
Artel, Jorge. *Poemas con botas y banderas*. Barranquilla: Universidad del Atlántico, 1972.
———. *Antología Poética*. Bogotá: ECOE Ediciones, 1979.

Arnoldo Palacios

Works Discussed
Las estrellas son negras, 1949. Bogotá: Editorial Revista Colombiana, 1971.
La selva y la lluvia. Moscú: Ediciones en Lenguas Extranjeras, 1958.

Other Works Consulted
J. M. D. "La segunda novela de Arnoldo Palacios." *Cromos* 89 (1960):45.
Johnson, Lemuel A. "The Dilemma of Presence in Black Diaspora Literature: A Comparativist Reading of Arnoldo Palacios' *Las estrellas son negras.*" *Afro-Hispanic Review* 1:1 (1982):3-10.
Monroy, Alvaro. "Un admirable esfuerzo: Arnoldo Palacios." *Cromos* 1681 (28 May 1949):6, 36.
Pérez Silva, Vicente. Review of *Las estrellas son negras*. *Noticias Culturales* 135 (1 April 1972):19-20.

Carlos Arturo Truque

Works Discussed
Granizada y otros cuentos. Bogotá: Espiral, 1953.
El día que terminó el verano y otros cuentos. Bogotá: Instituto Colombiano de Cultura, 1973.

Other Works Consulted
D'Orsonville, J. M. Alvarez. "Two Interviews." *Odyssey Review* 2:3 (1962):91-96.
Truque, Carlos Arturo. "De la artesanía a la gramática." *Boletín Cultural y Bibliográfico* 7:2 (1964):198-201.
———. "El cuento: una narración en desarrollo." *Letras Nacionales* 1:10 (1965):67-71.
———. "Proyecciones sociales de un ensayo: un texto inédito." *Revista de la Dirección de Divulgación* 16-17 (1977):13-23.
———. "La vocación y el medio: historia de un escritor." *Mito* 1:6 (1956):480-86.

Juan Zapata Olivella

Works Discussed
Historia de un joven negro. Port-au-Prince: Edición Haitana Le Natal, 1983.
Pisando el camino de ébano. Bogotá: Ediciones Lerner, 1984.

Other Works Consulted
Zapata Olivella, Juan. *Reseña de la primera candidatura negra a la presidencia de Colombia*. Port-au-Prince, Haiti: XPRESS, 1985.

Manuel Zapata Olivella

Works Discussed
Tierra mojada. Bogotá: Editorial Espiral, 1947.

La calle 10. Bogotá: Ediciones Casa de la Cultura, 1960.
Cuentos de muerte y libertad. Bogotá: Narradores Colombianos de hoy, 1961.
Corral de negros. Havana: Casa de las Américas, 1963. Published in Colombia as *Chambacú: Corral de negros*. Medellín: Editorial Bedout, 1963.
Detrás del rostro. Madrid: Aquilar, 1963.
En Chimá nace un santo. Barcelona: Seix Barral, 1964.
Changó, el gran putas. Bogotá: Editorial Oveja Negra, 1983.
El fusilamiento del diablo. Bogotá: Plaza y Janes, 1986.

Other Works Consulted
Anillo Sarmiento, Antonio. "La novelística comprometida de Manuel Zapata Olivella." Ph.D. dissertation, George Washington University, 1972.
Boglioli, François. *La Negritude et les problemes du noir dans l'oeuvre de Manuel Zapata Olivella*. Dakar-Abidjan: Les Nouvelles Editions Africaines, 1978.
Camacho Guizado, Eduardo. Review of *Detrás del rostro*. *Boletín Cultural y Bibliográfico* 7:10 (1964):2019-20.
Captain Hidalgo, Yvonne. "*Changó, el gran putas*." *Hispamerica* 14:41 (1985):124-25.
———. "Conversación con el doctor Manuel Zapata Olivella, Bogotá 1980; 1983." *Afro-Hispanic Review* 4:1 (1985):26-32.
———. "El espacio del tiempo en *Changó, el gran putas*." In *Ensayos de literatura colombiana*, ed. Raymond L. Williams, pp. 157-63. Bogotá: Plaza y Janes, 1985.
———. "The Realm of Possibilities: A Comparative Analysis of Selected Works by Alejo Carpentier and Manuel Zapata Olivella." Ph.D. dissertation, Stanford University, 1984.
Caruso, Wanda. "*La calle 10*." Bogotá: Instituto Caro y Cuervo, 1964.
Cuervo Escobar, Julio Enrique. "*Detrás del rostro*: una acusación a la sociedad." Bogotá: Instituto Caro y Cuervo, 1964.
Doerr, Richard Paul. "La magia como dinámica de evasión en la novelística de Manuel Zapata Olivella." Ph.D. dissertation, University of Colorado, 1973.
Durán Salcedo, Gloria. "Aspectos costumbristas: en *Tierra mojada*, novela de Manuel Zapata Olivella." Bogotá: Instituto Caro y Cuervo, 1967.
González, Francisco José. Review of *Tierra mojada*. *Revista Javeriana* 29:142 (1948):114.
Herrera Soto, Roberto. "Zapata Olivella o las perspectivas de la negritud

en las Américas." *La República/Suplemento Dominical*, 18 March 1984, pp. 1-12.

Lewis, Marvin A. Review of *Changó, el gran putas*. Association of Caribbean Studies *Newsletter* (fall 1984):4-5.

———. "*En Chimá nace un santo*: Myth and Violence." *Kentucky Romance Quarterly* 25:2 (1978):21-26.

———. "La trayectoria novelística de Manuel Zapata Olivella: de la opresión a la liberación." In *Ensayos de literatura colombiana*, ed. Raymond L. Williams, pp. 137-48. Bogotá: Plaza y Janes, 1985.

Paez de Rivera, Fanny. "Los personajes reales en la novelística de Manuel Zapata Olivella." Monografía para optar al título de licenciada en Filosofía y Humanismo. Bogotá: Universidad Santo Tomás de Aquino, 1978.

Rodríguez, Agustín. Review of *La calle 10*. *Boletín Cultural y Bibliográfico* 3:7 (1960):451.

Ruiz Camacho, Rubén. "*Detrás del rostro*, una novela ejemplar." *Boletín Cultural y Bibliográfico* 8:1 (1965):105-6.

Smart, Ian. Review of *Changó, el gran putas*. *Afro-Hispanic Review* 3:2 (1984):31-32.

———. "*Changó, el gran putas*, una nueva novela poemática." In *Ensayos de literatura colombiana*, ed. Raymond L. Williams, pp. 149-56. Bogotá: Plaza y Janes, 1985.

Sohn, Guansu. "La novela colombiana de protesta social." Ph.D. dissertation, University of Oklahoma, 1976.

Williams, Raymond L., and Gómez, Gilberto. "Interview with Manuel Zapata Olivella." *Hispania* 67 (1984):657-58.

Index

A

Afro-Colombian, defined, 2
Amis, Barry: doctoral dissertation on Colombian literature, 11
Aretz, Isabel: on African influence on Latin American music and dance, 55-56
Artel, Jorge: works, 1, 63; themes, 63-64; *No es la muerte, es el morir,* 63-72; "Poemas con botas y banderas," 69; "Poema para no ser olvidado," 70; "Este duro salitre en mi pecho," 70-71
Auctorial narration, defined, 63

B

Barthold, Bonnie: concepts of time in *Changó, el gran putas,* 113
Belsey, Catherine: on ideology and literature, 7-8
Betancur, Belisario: and Colombian violence, 66
Bioho, Benkos: as portrayed in *Changó, el gran putas,* 115-16
Bousoño, Carlos: definition of the Romantic system, 74-75, 80
Brathwaite, Edward Kamau: African Literatures in the Caribbean, 2
Bronx, Humberto: criticism of *Las estrellas son negras,* 17-18
Brushwood, John S., 15; criticism of *La Calle 10,* 98

C

Camacho Guizado, Eduardo: criticism of *Detrás del rostro,* 107
Carpentier, Alejo: *The Kingdom of This World* as it relates to *Changó, el gran putas,* 118
Caruso, Wanda: criticism of *La Calle 10,* 98
Changó: characterized, 56, 112
Chocó Pacific Mining Company: as instrument of exploitation in Colombia, 27-29, 32; presence in *La selva y la lluvia,* 28, 32
Culler, Jonathan: definition of intertextuality, 5-6; cultural intertextuality, 118
Cultural intertextuality, 14, 118
Cumbia, Afro-Colombian dance, 91
Currulao, Afro-Colombian dance, 55-56

D

D'Orsonville, J. M. Alvarez: interview with Carlos Arturo Truque, 39-40
de Friedemann, Nina: on Afro-Colombian literature, 15
Dorfman, Ariel: categories of violence, 8-10
Dorsinville, Max: exile and the black experience, 4
Durán Salcedo, Gloria: criticism of *Tierra mojada,* 87

E

Eagleton, Terry: definition of ideology, 6-7; on literature and society, 13; on literary production and ideology, 35, 62
Eile, Stanislaw: definition of auctorial narration, 63

139

F

Franco, Jean: on research priorities in Latin American literary scholarship, 123
Furst, Lillian: definition of Naturalism, 18, 20

G

Gaitán, Jorge Eliecer: assassination of, 8; and La Violencia, 8, 10; in *Las estrellas son negras,* 31; in *No es la muerte, es el morir,* 64, 66; in *Poemas con botas y banderas,* 69–70; violence related to in *La Calle 10,* 100–102, 127
Gamín: street urchin experience in *Detrás del rostro,* 108–12
Gómez, Gilberto: interview with Manuel Zapata Olivella regarding *Changó, el gran putas,* 113–14
González, Francisco José: criticism of *Tierra mojada,* 86–87
Guerin, Wilfred: archetypal patterns, 53
Guillén, Nicolás: in the cultural intertext of *Pisando el camino de ébano,* 83

H

Hughes, Langston: in the cultural intertext of *Pisando el camino de ébano,* 83
Hutcheon, Linda: definition of parody, 77

I

Ideology: defined, 6–7
Ilie, Paul: definition of inner exile, 4
Intertextuality, 5
Isaacs, Jorge: *María* as intertext for *Historia de un joven negro,* 73–74

J

Jackson, Richard: Authenticity in Latin American literature, 3–4; on Maximo the activist protagonist of *Chambacú, corral de negros,* 107; perspectives of black literature, 120

K

Kirsner, Robert: on Colombian novels of "La Violencia," 122
Kooreman, Thomas: on the "Bogotazo," 121

L

Leal, Luis: on Carlos Arturo Truque, 38–39
Lernoux, Penny: and Liberation Theology, 67
Liberation Theology: in *No es la muerte, es el morir,* 67

M

Mackandal, François: as portrayed in *Changó, el gran putas,* 116–17
McMurray, George: discussion of the Spanish American short story, 41, 51
Madrid Malo, Nestor: development of the Colombian novel, 12
Malcolm X: as portrayed in *Changó, el gran putas,* 118
Miscegenation: in *Las estrellas son negras,* 23; in *Tierra mojada,* 88–90, 114
Monroy, Alvaro: criticism of *Las estrellas son negras,* 17
Montana Cuéllar, Diego: on

Index

Colombian troop involvement in Korea, 104-5

N

Naturalism, defined, 18, 20

P

Paez de Rivera, Fanny: criticism of *Tierra mojada*, 87-88
Palacios, Arnoldo: works, 1, 15; themes, 15-16; *Las estrellas son negras*, 16-25; *La selva y la lluvia*, 26-37
Parody: in *Historia de un joven negro*, 77
Pederson, Carl: doctoral dissertation on Colombian literature, 11
Pérez Silva, Vicente: criticism of *Las estrellas son negras*, 17
Pupo Walker, Enrique, 38

R

Rodríquez, Agustín: criticism of *La Calle 10*, 97-98
Romanticism: in *Historia de un joven negro*, 74-77
Ruiz Camacho, Rubén: criticism of *Detrás del rostro*, 108

S

Skrine, Peter: definition of naturalism, 20, 118
Smart, Ian: criticism of *Changó, el gran putas*, 118
Suárez Rondón, Gerardo: criticism of *Detrás del rostro*, 107

T

Torres, Camilo: as religious martyr, in *No es la muerte, es el morir*, 66-68
Truque, Carlos Arturo: works, 1, 38; themes, 38-39; theory of the short story, 39-40; relationship between literature and society, 42; *Granizada y otros cuentos*, 43-50; "Porque así era la gente," 43-44; "La gafas oscuras," 44; "Martín encuentra dos razones," 44-45; "La noche de San Silvestre," 45-46; "La muerte tuvo cara y sello," 46; "Granizada," 46-47; "Sangre en el llano," 47-48; "La Fuga," 48; "Lo triste de vivir así," 48-49; *El día que terminó el verano y otros cuentos*, 50-62; "El día que terminó el verano," 51-54; "Sonatina para dos tambores," 54-56; "El encuentro," 56; "Fucú," 56-57; "Reveille," 57-58; "Dos hombres," 58-59; "El misterio," 59-60
Turner, Nat: as character in *Changó, el gran putas*, 117

V

Violence: as literary concept, 8-10; in Colombian politics, 8; as theme, 31, 64, 66, 69-70, 100-102, 121

W

Williams, Raymond: definition of ideology, 6-7; characteristics of ideology, 16; interview with Manuel Zapata Olivella regarding *Changó, el gran putas*, 113-14

Z

Zapata Olivella, Juan: works, 1-2, 72; themes, 72; *Historia de un joven negro*, 72-81; *Pisando el camino de ébano*, 81-84

Zapata Olivella, Manuel:
works, 1–2, 85; themes,
85–86; *Tierra mojada*, 86–94;
En Chimá nace un santo,
94–97; *La Calle 10*, 97–102;
Chambacú, corral de negros,
102–7; *Detrás del rostro*,
107–12; *Changó, el gran
putas*, 112–19; *El fusilamiento del diablo*, 85, 128